Super Kids

In

30 Minutes A Day

by

Karen U. Kwiatkowski, M.S., M.A.

Robert D. Reed Publishers • San Francisco, California

Robert D. Reed Publishers
750 La Playa, Suite 647 • San Francisco, CA 94121
1-800-PR-GREEN • Fax: (408) 255-8830

Book Cover by Pamela D. Jacobs & Destiny Design
Typesetting by Pamela D. Jacobs
Layout by Ragani Harris

Library of Congress Cataloging-in-Publication Data

Kwiatkowski, Karen U.
    Super kids in 30 minutes a day / by Karen U. Kwiatkowski.
       p.   cm.
    Includes bibliographical references.
    ISBN 1-885003-06-4 : $9.95
    1. Child rearing. 2. Parenting. I. Title. II. Title: Super kids in
thirty minutes a day.
HQ769.K92   1995
649' .1--dc20

            94-43565
            CIP

Manufactured, Typeset, and Printed in the United States of America

Dedication

To Katie, G.J., Betsy, Michael, and most of all, Hap.

Contents

Acknowledgements

I am grateful to the White House Office of National Service for permission to reprint examples of volunteerism for children, as published under the Thousand Points of Light program.

Introduction

Kids need more from their parents than ever before, while we parents seem to have less and less to provide. And it's not just time, it's the "what", too. What should we be doing for our kids? There is a lot of advice and discussion going on in our communities and the media, and we keep hearing about family values — but whose family are they talking about? What should we in our own little microcosm of parent and child do to end up with a kid who is happy, positive, responsible, capable, caring, kind and good? What do we do to help our kid achieve — to have the kind of child who can seize the day and his or her future?

This book provides some ideas on how we can foster our children's growth, as well as a constructive parent-child relationship through using a few simple steps. You don't have to be an expert in child psychology, in fact, you don't have to be an expert in anything. In fact, a lot of what's in this book will seem obvious — after you've read it — when before you didn't see it at all. As a side benefit, a lot of things we can do and home environments we can create are real time savers for us as parents. Each topic in this book has an estimated time cost (or time savings) as well as a resource cost. So you'll know what you're getting into beforehand.

I have four kids of my own, ranging from three to ten years old, and I have had a full time job outside the home since before I had children. Before you think I'm just "too much," you need to know that I have a husband who has stayed home with these kids since the oldest was a baby. A lot of what a man brings to child-rearing and household management is well beyond the American paradigm of "motherhood" — and it is in watching him, and our family, that I have gleaned some basic knowledge on what things both save time and are extremely effective in producing good, creative, smart and healthy kids. Every family can improve its environment, and every kid's potential can be expanded — and this book shows how in less than thirty planned minutes a day!

SECTION ONE

NURTURING

nurture: 1. to promote the development of by providing nourishment, support, encouragement, etc., during the stages of growth, 2. to bring up; train; educate.

Webster's Encyclopedic Unabridged
Dictionary of the English Language

1. Breastfeed Your Baby

Time Cost:	Five minutes saved per feeding; up to forty minutes saved per day.
Resource Cost:	None. Up to $2,000 a year saved in cost of formula.

Human breast milk is the biological nourishment for babies. Breastfeeding provides the best mix of critical nerve development nutrients for the newborn. However, only about half of the women in the United States breastfeed their babies at all, and as few as one in five continue past six months. Among women in reduced economic situations the percentages who breastfeed are even lower.

Why would parents want to purchase an expensive chemical concoction when breastmilk is basically free, superior in food value and digestibility, and ready on demand (no bottles to sterilize or formula to mix and heat)? Studies have shown that one reason may be related to the hospital or physician distribution of formula (both free samples and coupons for free or reduced price formulas) to new mothers. Another reason is lack of institutionalized prenatal instruction and training in breastfeeding techniques and practices. A third has to do with the misconception that working mothers cannot or even should not breastfeed their infants.

Perhaps Americans on average are a little too prudish and in awe of modern science and technology to really feel strongly about breastfeeding when we have such a high-tech alternative — although the exhausted mother or father mixing and heating a bottle at 3 a.m. with a squalling babe in the bedroom may wonder at the high-technology of it all! In any case — breastfeeding your baby, for as much and as long as you possibly can, is the first step towards raising a great kid. Why do I say this? It's not because breastfeeding is better for baby development (although it is), or because it helps you save for college or a vacation (although it can), or because it makes you closer to your baby than bottlefeeding (no reason it must), or because it is convenient and ready whenever required. It is because in breastfeeding your baby you give totally of yourself to your child. You provide something to your child that no one else can. In this special way you, the mother of a wonderful and amazing little person, become aware of your importance. This awareness of your importance to your baby is preparation for your role as this baby grows. It is a confidence builder that you as Mother need to have and to recognize, because you will need that confidence as the strange and wonderful process of growth goes on. And it will go on and it will go quickly and you will not pass this way again. That's why you should breastfeed your baby.

If you have breastfed your baby, good work. If you are expecting a baby anytime in the future, learn everything you can about breastfeeding, and make a commitment to do it for your baby. If you did not breastfeed your child or children, do not despair. If you are reading this book, you have already shown a concern for your child's welfare that warrants well for his or her success.

For more information on breastfeeding:

Recommended Books:

Breastfeeding by Janice Presser and B. Brewer (Knopf, 1983)

Breastfeeding Your Baby by Sheila Kitzinger (Knopf, 1989)

Breastfeeding: Something Special for Mother and Baby by Toni Berg (New Futures, 1992)

Successful Breastfeeding: A Complete Step-by-Step Guide to Nursing Your Baby by Nancy Dana and Anne Price (Simon and Schuster, 1985)

Working Woman's Guide to Breastfeeding by Nancy Dana and Anne Price (Meadowbrook, 1987)

Organizations:

La Leche League Intl.
9616 Minneapolis Avenue
P. O. Box 1209
Franklin Park, IL 60131-8209
(708) 455-7730 or
1 (800)-LA-LECHE (525-3243)

Human Lactation Ctr.
666 Sturges Highway
Westport, CT 06880
(203) 259-5995

2. Get The Lead Out

Time Cost:	20 minutes a month
Resource Cost:	Zero to $100

*L*ead ingestion, through the stomach or through inhalation, is linked to health problems and learning deficiencies in children. Lead can be found all around us, and young and unborn children are especially susceptible to longterm damage including lowered IQs and behavioral problems. Possible sources of lead include paint, inks in newspapers and magazines, pewter, solder, pottery, lead crystal, old plumbing, fishing sinkers and weights, and hobby supplies associated with ceramics, stained glass-making, renovation and automotive repair. Don't panic, but be aware. You keep lead away from your child when you:

∞ Eliminate your child's access to peeling paint inside and outside the home.

∞ Keep children from mouthing painted items.

∞ Wash your child's hands and face frequently, especially before eating.

∞ Wash toys and pacifiers frequently.

∞ Keep your child from chewing printed paper.

∞ Use cold tap water for drinking, cooking, and mixing formula and juices. Let the tap run until cold, especially when the tap has been unused for six or more hours. Most pre-1989 homes have pipes joined with lead solder, which can leach from the pipes into the water.

∞ Don't store food in pottery, ceramics, or imported cans. Be especially careful not to store acidic foods or juices in ceramic-ware.

∞ Don't microwave china or other pottery containers unless they are marked microwave-safe. High risk potteries include old china, home-made or hand-crafted china, highly decorated, multi-colored glazed pottery, or pottery with corroded glaze.

∞ Make sure home exposures are not occurring from parental occupations or hobbies. Change or clean dusty or dirty clothes before going home.

∞ Ensure your child eats regular, nutritious meals. More lead is absorbed on an empty stomach.

∞ Feed your child a diet high in iron. This slows lead absorption.

∞ Get professional advice concerning possible lead risk before renovating any old painted surfaces.

You can test for lead in your home using inexpensive lead test kits. Some sources include the following:

Leadcheck Swabs
HybriVet Systems, Inc
P.O. Box 1210
Framingham, MA 01701
1-800-262-LEAD

The Frandon Lead Alert Kit
Frandon Enterprises
511 North 48th Street
Seattle, WA 98103
1-800-359-9000

For more information on lead sources, lead poisoning, or related issues:

Books and Pamphlets:

Preventing Lead Poisoning in Young Children, (CDC), Washington, D.C., U.S. Department of Health and Human Services, 1991

The Hour of Lead: A Brief History of Lead Poisoning in the United States, Washington, D.C., Environmental Defense Funds, 1992

Poisoning our Children: Surviving in a Toxic World by Nancy Sokol Green (Noble, 1991)

The Citizen's Guide to Lead: Uncovering a Hidden Health Hazard (Seven Hills Book Distributors, 1989)

"Getting the Lead Out" Write for this free 6-page FDA booklet from Consumer Information Center, P.O. Box 100, Pueblo, CO 81002

"Home Buyer's Guide to Environmental Hazards" 41 page booklet which covers lead and other environmental risks and what to do about them. Send fifty cents to Consumer Information Center, P.O. Box 100, Pueblo, CO 81002

Organizations:

National Lead Information
Center Hotline
1-800-LEAD-FYI
(1-800-532-3394)

U.S. Consumer Products Safety
Commission
Washington, D.C. 20207
(301) 504-0580

Alliance to End Childhood Lead Poisoning
600 Pennsylvania Avenue, SE
Suite 100
Washington, D.C. 20003
(202) 543-1147

Centers for Disease Control (CDC) Lead Poisoning and Prevention Branch
1600 Clifton Road, NE
Atlanta, GA 30333

3. Lose The Playpen

Time Cost :	1 hour a month
Resource Cost:	Zero to $1000 a year, if you have babies or toddlers

Imagine your office or desk with an invisible force field surrounding it. You can work with the limited supplies in your office, but you rely on people outside to bring you everything and anything else. The world you see beyond the invisible barrier is filled with activity and color and sound and interesting objects. You are in a continual mode of waiting for something to come your way. You become practiced at waiting, and in time you may become very good at it. You may also experience frustration, and in time you will learn to passively cope with that as well.

Your baby lives in this world, and never moreso than when he or she is awake in a playpen. A baby experiences many barriers of communication and action, and each are meant to be overcome. Normal barriers for your baby are all learning opportunities. For example, your child wants food or comfort, and he or she will cry to get your attention. Later, the child wants a certain drink or toy or activity, and will learn to identify his or her needs verbally and physically. These communication and action barriers are skill related. Playpens, or any of the other types of child restraining devices are, contrarily, barriers that are not meant to be overcome. They are not learning opportunities, but instead parental conveniences.

Think about the items in your baby's life that constitute parental conveniences — consider playpens, baby walkers, strollers, and baby swings. Then consider how often you use these devices, and consider honestly if you can make better choices for the time your baby is awake. A simple goal is to cut the time your child spends restrained or constrained, during his or her waking hours by half. To meet this goal, childproof your home appropriately and keep it safe for both the child and for your property.

You will also need to reprioritize the things you do when your baby is awake. Plan on socializing with your child in your home. Treat him or her as a guest, invited over for an hour or two. Would you relegate a guest to a back room and lock the door while you prepare dinner or watch the news? Or would you instead postpone those chores or involve the guest in the activity? Consider your baby as a guest in your house, the best kind of guest — the one who doesn't notice if the house is clean or neat, and loves you totally and unconditionally. If you look at it this way, you will agree that we, as parents and caretakers, are most blessed. Return the favor to your baby by reducing "convenience" restraints and childproofing your home.

Basic child safety devices for the home can be found in just about any local store. For more information:

Books:

Safe Kids: A Complete Child Safety Handbook and Resource Guide for Parents by Vivian K. Fancher (Wiley, 1991)

Childproofing Checklist: A Parent's Guide to Accident Prevention by Mary Metzger and Cinthya P. Whittaker (Doubleday, 1988)

Organizations:

U.S. Consumer Product Safety Commission
Washington, D.C. 20207
(Write for a list of free safety publications)

The National Safe Kids Campaign
111 Michigan Avenue, NW
Washington, D.C. 20010

Parenting Publications of America
12715 Pathfinder Lane
San Antonio, TX 78230
(210) 492-3886

Mail order sources for child safety items include the following:

Baby Safety Specialists, Inc.
2139 N. University Drive, Suite 196
Coral Springs, FL 33071-9966
(305) 341-9072

Perfectly Safe
7245 Whipple Avenue, N.W.
North Canton, OH 44720
(216) 494-4366
1 (800) 837-KIDS (837-5437)

Child Safety Catalog
KinderKraft, Inc
P.O. Box 5433
Arlington, VA 22205
(703) 841-1902

F&H Child Safety Company
P.O. Box 2228
Evansville, IN 47714
(812) 479-8485

The Safety Zone Catalog
Hanover, PA 17333-0019
1-800-999-3030

New York Babyproofing
Manhattan, New York
(212) 362-1262

International Cushioned Products, Inc
202-8360 Bridgeport Road
Richmond, BC V6X 3C7 Canada
1-800-TUB-SOFT (1-800-882-7638)

Safety by Design
P.O. Box 4312
Great Neck, NY 11023
(516) 488-5395

The Right Start Catalog
Right Start Plaza
5334 Sterling Center Drive
Westlake Village, CA 91361-4627
1-800-LITTLE-1 (1-800-548-8531)

4. Make Music!

Time Cost:	2 minutes a day
Resource Cost:	None for most families

*E*very home with children already has music — children's voices, and laughter, and singing. A baby is born with a sense of hearing already well developed, and baby knows mother's voice and heartbeat. Sound is a sensory world that is waiting to be explored, so provide your baby and your older children with plenty of sound variety. Simple ways to do this include:

> • Sing or whistle while you work or relax around the house or in the car.

> • Play the radio during the day and evening. Keep it on, tuned to a music-oriented station, instead of relying on the TV for background noise.

• Play tapes, CDs, and records for yourself with your baby and older children. All kinds of music can be checked out at the local library at no cost. Make music a family habit.

• Make sure your toddler and older childen have a small tape player and their own tapes for children's music, poems, and stories. When a parent goes away on a trip without the kids, make tapes like these ahead of time or send them home in the mail.

• Encourage your children to make music. Sing with them, and compliment their singing and music-making.

• Provide opportunities for making music: This includes lessons when appropriate or possible, and opportunities to make and play home-made instruments.

• Take your children to a concert at least once a year. Whether this is your high school holiday choir, or church celebration, or an orchestra at the park or coliseum, make an effort to do it.

For more information:

Books:

Music for Children by Doreen Hall and Donald Hines

How to Grow a Music Lover: Helping Your Child Discover and Enjoy the World of Music by Cheri Fuller (Shaw Publications, 1993)

Organizations/Periodicals:

Music Teachers National Association
617 Vine Street, Suite 1432
Cincinnati, OH 45202

Early Childhood Music
Miss Jackie Music Company
10001 El Monte
Overland Park, KS 66207
(Bi-monthly newsletter)

Sources:

**Children's Book and
Music Center**
2500 Santa Monica Blvd
Santa Monica, CA 90404

Music for Little People
Box 516
Montpelier, VT 05601
1-800-223-MFLP (223-6357)

5. Read!

Time Cost:	10 to 15 minutes a day
Resource Cost:	$0 - $50 a year

Your child should read or be read to every day. Read to and with your children before or after dinner, during the meal, before bedtime or in the morning before school. Read between television shows and during TV commercials. Consider reading a natural pleasure, and read yourself. If you don't find reading a pleasure, improve your reading skills and/or your choice of materials. American culture is print-oriented. What other cultures share through "oral" traditions, ours shares largely through books and print media.

Success in our society depends on information — the ability to get it, make sense of it, and use it. Successful democracy in our country can survive only with the participation of a nation of readers. Reading IS that important.

How do we build reading into our lives? There are a multitude of opportunities, but here are a few to get you started and keep you going:

∞ Get library cards for every member of the family. Visit the library often, with and without your children. Build the library into your routine weekly stops.

∞ Read to your kids while doing other things (waiting for the microwave to "ding" with breakfast, lunch or supper, while soaking in the tub (either you or the kids), during TV advertisements (turn the volume down and pick up a book, magazine, or newspaper).

∞ When shopping with your children, read the food labels, store advertisements and signs. Read billboards or street signs on the way to and from the store.

∞ Keep books in every room of the house, both your books and your kids' books. If you are a neatnik, get wicker baskets or install wall mounted book shelves, but be sure to have books easily available throughout the house.

∞ Keep books and magazines in the car. Rotate them periodically and make use of them when riding and waiting in the car.

∞ Make a rule that for each video your child watches, a book (or two) is read either to or by him or her.

∞ Have older siblings read aloud to their younger ones, and vice versa.

∞ Give your children their own magazine subscriptions.

∞ Read out loud from books, magazines, and newspapers to your significant other, and to the children.

∞ Own your own books. In addition to the library books that you must return, your house should have books for kids and adults that are yours to keep. I recommend used books, either from library book swap racks, yard and garage sales, library sales, and thrift shops. For children's books, let your friends who have older kids know that you are looking for books for your kids to both borrow and keep. There is a notion in our society that says possessions should be new and disposable. Recycling children's books can sometimes go against the grain of many mothers and fathers. I would argue for actively acquiring used books for your kids for a number of reasons, but mainly these three:

1) It makes the book money go many times further — more books and more variety, exposure, and diversity in the reading material for the investment.

2) It eliminates the mother-, father-, and grandparent-caused anxiety that is a direct reaction to Junior's artwork on page nine of the wonderfully illustrated $29.99 book you just brought home from the bookstore, or the three-year old's tantrum that resulted in a "valuable" book thrown down the stairs. Certainly, we don't want our children to disrespect property, but the value is mostly in the book's content, not its binding. If we communicate that reading is for special occasions only, or in any way betray our children's curiosity or childish judgement relative to books, we do our children a disservice.

3) Reusing books means recycling books, both the charm and the joy of the stories, as well as the physical paper and materials. If you are not sure you want to own books that someone else's children have read, just think of it as saving a tree.

For more information on the encouragement of reading:

Books:

The Read-Aloud Handbook, Revised Ed. by Jim Trelease (Penguin Books, 1985)

The New Read-Aloud Handbook by Jim Trelease (Penguin Books, 1989)

Raise a Reader! by Jim Trelease (Viking Penguin, 1990)

Hey! Listen to This: Stories to Read Aloud by Jim Trelease (Viking Penguin, 1992)

Read All About It by Jim Trelease (Penguin Books, 1993)

Family Reading by Ellen Goldsmith and Ruth Hanel (New York: New Readers Press, 1990)

The RIF Guide to Encouraging Young Readers by Ruth Graves (Doubleday, 1987)

A variety of helpful pamphlets are available from the Consumer Information Center. Write to them at Consumer Information Center-2D, P.O. Box 100, Pueblo, CO 81002 and request any or all of the following pamphlets:

"Becoming a Nation of Readers: What Parents Can Do." A 36 page booklet, for fifty cents, with activities and techniques for adults to help children of all ages build reading skills.

"Books for Children." A 23-page booklet, for $1, listing more than 100 of the best children's books recently published for preschool through junior high school.

"Help Your Child Become a Good Reader." five-page, fifty-cent booklet that describes how to help your child understand reading fundamentals through suggestions that center around everyday occurrences and items.

"Helping Your Child Use the Library." A 21-page, fifty-cent booklet with tips on getting children of all ages interested in books.

"Timeless Classics." A four-page, fifty-cent booklet listing nearly 400 children's books published before 1960.

Organizations:

American Library Association
Public Information Office
50 E. Huron Street
Chicago, IL 60611

Reading is Fundamental (RIF)
600 Maryland Avenue, SW Suite 500
P.O. Box 23444
Washington, D.C. 20060
(202) 287-3220

Barbara Bush Foundation
for Family Literacy
1002 Wisconsin Avenue NW
Washington, D.C. 2007
(202) 338-2006

International Reading
Association
800 Barksdale Road
P.O. Box 8139
Newark, DE 19714-8139
(302) 731-1600

Parent's Choice Foundation
P.O. Box 185
Wabon, MA 02168
(617) 965-5913

Books for children are readily available in libraries and local bookstores. Mail order sources for children's books include the following:

A Child's Collection of
Wonderful Books
155 Avenue of the Americas
New York, NY 10013
(212) 691-7266

Gryphon House
P.O. Box 207
Beltsville, MD 20704-0207
(301) 595-9500
1-800-638-0928

Better Beginning Catalog
345 N. Main Street
W. Hartford, CT 06117
(203) 236-4907

Books of Wonder
132 7th Avenue
New York, NY 10011
(212) 989-3270

Children's Book & Music Ctr.
2500 Santa Monica Blvd
Santa Monica, CA 90404

Chinaberry Book Service
2780 Via Orange Way, Suite B
Spring Valley, CA 91978
(619) 670-5200
1 (800) 776-2242

**Children's Small Press
Collection**

719 N. 4th Avenue
Ann Arbor, MI 48104
(313) 668-8056
1-800-221-8056

Gleanings

60 Priorway Drive
Novelty, OH 44072
(216) 321-0214

6. "Watch" TV

Time Cost:	5 to 20 minutes a week
Resource Cost:	$0 (some electricity may be saved) to over $100 (if you purchase a television lock device)

t has been widely reported that outdoor and physical activity levels for children has been steadily dropping, while passive activities such as TV viewing, computer and video-game playing are on the rise. Also widely reported and observed is the questionable quality of television programming. In fact, with the ever expanding amount of choice we have on television via cable access, there are many good things for our children to watch on television. The key is choosing and managing the television, and preventing the television from managing us and our children.

What can you do to "watch" your children's TV diet? Here are a few ideas:

∞ Do not automatically allow your children to watch so-called "children's shows." Excellent examples of shows "for children" that are not really appropriate for them (and in any case add no value) are many of the cartoon shows, including the popular animated "The Simpsons" and Saturday morning cartoons that are rehashed PG, PG-13, and R-rated movies (Beetlejuice, Batman, Ninja Turtles). What can you do? Watch them once yourself, then decide if the show is watchable, or off-limits.

∞ Don't allow homework to be done in front of the television, unless the TV is turned off.

∞ Set a daily or weekly limit on TV viewing for each child in the family (and also for each parent!). Consider a one to three hour limit per day, but allow each family member to select the shows on which they'd like to apply their TV credits. The TV shows that family members watch need to be from the list of "approved" shows.

∞ Have certain times when the TV is simply left turned off. This should include dinnertime, and other meal-times, and when homework is being done.

∞ Eliminate television sets in children's bedrooms.

∞ Have your children "earn" TV credits by doing household chores, or completing homework, or writing letters, or reading a book, or helping a sibling or a neighbor.

∞ Use the VCR to tape shows for later viewing — the effort itself is often enough to separate those shows worth watching and those that aren't.

∞ Turn TV commercials into opportunities for critical thinking and family discussion.

• Keep a list of the number, length, and type of TV commercials viewed by channel. Have all family members help document, and then periodically discuss what the information means. Are certain groups of people being targeted for certain shows? Do people really get as many colds and headaches as the commercials would indicate? How can we confirm or deny what is being presented as "fact"?

• Establish a list of questions (write them down and keep them near the TV set) that the kids can ask about commercials they see. The list could include the following, for starters:

1) What is the commercial trying to say about the product?

2) Do I want to buy this product? Why?

3) Do I need this product? When would I need it?

4) Did the commercial really describe the product? For example, did the soda commercial talk about the taste of the drink? Did the car commercial tell how well the car runs and how long it lasts? Did the clothing ad discuss comfort, durability, style, and quality? How did the perfume commercial describe the product's scent?

∞ Watch the evening news together, and be available to discuss what it means to you and to your children. Some of the scariest stuff is injected into our homes every night via the local, national, and international news. Both in terms of subject matter and visual display, some of what is on the news can be alarming and disturbing. Be prepared to talk to your children about the news, and be sure to have a national or world map, or preferably a globe on top of the TV, to show your children where they are in relation to where the hurricane, flood, war, explosion, or outbreak of disease is occurring. If you can't watch the TV news with your children, or you are unwilling to discuss what they see, don't let your younger children watch at all.

∞ If you are not happy with what you are seeing on TV, write a letter to the local station and also to the networks.

You may have ideas on when certain shows are broadcast, or the lack of positive stories on the local newscast, or you are displeased with the level of violence, or rough language, or lack of appropriate children's fare, or perhaps you're happy with something the stations or the networks are doing. WRITE A LETTER! Type or print it if you can, keep it concise and no more than one page, and don't be cruel, just communicate! To get mileage from what you have, make copies of the same letter and send information copies to the local station, the network, and your state or national representative. To write your local stations, just look in the phone book for the addresses. To write the major networks, you can use the following addresses:

ABC: President, ABC Entertainment
2040 Avenue of the Starts
Century City, CA 90067

CBS: President, CBS Entertainment
7800 Beverly Blvd
Los Angeles, CA 90036

NBC: President, NBC West
3000 W. Alameda
Burbank, CA 91523

FOX: Fox Entertainment
Box 900
Beverly Hills, CA 90213

Federal Communications Commission (FCC)
1919 M Street, NW
Washington, D.C. 20554

∞ Work with your local cable company, and know what you're getting. If you are unhappy with the cable choice or purchase combinations, say so. Perhaps there is a "family" combo you can get, or perhaps one can be offered by your local cable company. If you are not happy with what you are getting on cable, consider cancelling unnecessary channels. Look into what your local cable company can offer on a pay-per-view basis as an alternative to a multitude of not-so-appropriate offerings.

∞ Invest in a TV lock-out device. The devices range from simple power-key lock devices to more complicated time calculator devices. For example:

"The Switch" Childproof box that controls electricity to the TV set. Price: $21.95 plus shipping. Call 1-800-535-5845 for information.

"TV Allowance" Parents can program an amount of time that children can watch each week. Each child receives a four digit code to turn the set on. As they watch, their "accounts" are debited, and when their allotment is up, the TV shuts itself off. Price: $99.00 plus shipping. Call 1-800-231-4410 for information.

"SuperVision" This device turns the TV on and off for two different time periods each day, so parents can control both how much time the children spend watching, as well as what they see. The device also tallies total TV time. Price: $79.95 plus shipping. Call 1-800-845-1911 for information.

Some sources for information on how to better critique and manage TV:

Books and Pamphlets:

Use TV to Your Child's Advantage by Dorothy G. Singer, Jerome L. Singer, and Dian M. Zuckerman. (Acropolis Books, 1990)

TV: Becoming Unglued by Addie Jurs (Robert Erdmann Publ., 1992)

Breaking Your Child's TV Addiction: A Guide for Parents by David Demers (Marquette Books, 1989)

"TV with Books Completes the Picture." This six page booklet suggests activities related to TV viewing that encourages reading and writing, as well as a list of resources. Free from the Consumer Information Center-2D, P.O. Box 100, Pueblo, CO 81002.

"What Parents Should Know about TV" Write to Channing L. Bete Co., Inc., 200 State Road, South Deerfield, MA 01373.

"A Guide for Parents" Write to Educational Improvement Center - South, 207 Delsea Drive, R.D. 4, Box 209, Sewell, NJ 08080.

"Sex on Television" by D.L. Green. Write to Health Care of Southeastern Mass, Inc., 728 Brockton Ave, Abington, MA 02351.

"Parents, Children, and TV" by Dorothy G. Singer and Helen B. Kelly. Write to the National PTA, 700 N. Rush Street, Chicago, IL 60611.

"The Prime-Time Primer" Write to Health Care of Southeastern Mass, Inc., 728 Brockton Ave, Abington, MA 02351.

"The Family Learning Guide — Television Viewing Write to Family Learning, 19 Davis Drive, Belmont, CA 94002.

"Your Child and TV" by Jerome L. and Dorothy G. Singer, Write to Educational Services, Head Start Bureau Administration for Children, Youth, and Families, P.O. Box 1182, Washington, D.C. 20201.

Organizations:

Action for Children's Television (ACT)
20 University Road
Cambridge, MA 02168
(617) 876-6620

National Coalition for Television Violence
P.O. Box 2157
Champaign, IL 61825
(217) 384-1920

Viewers for Quality Television
P.O. Box 195
Fairfax Station, VA 22039

Center for Media and Values
1962 S. Shenandoah Street
Los Angeles, CA 90034
(310) 559-2944

Society for the Eradication of Television
Box 10491
Oakland, CA 94610-0491
(415) 530-2056

Yale University Family Television Research & Consultation Center
405 Temple Street
New Haven, CT 06511

Center for the Study of Commercialism
1875 Connecticut Avenue, NW, Suite 300
Wahington, D.C. 20009-5728
(202) 332-9110

Playright (Video game newsletter for parents)
(415) 349-4300
1-800-238-1313

KIDSNET
Consumer Information Center
Dept 58
Pueblo, CO 81009

Center for Media Education
1511 K Street NW
Suite 518
Washington, D.C. 20005
(202) 628-2620

Media Foundation
1243 West 7th Avenue
Vancouver, B.C. V6H 1B7
Canada
(604) 736-9401

Parent's Choice Foundation
P.O. Box 185
Newton, MA 02168

7. Establish A Bedtime Routine

Time Cost:	Once established, saves up to 60 minutes a day, based on your previous record for getting them to bed.
Resource Cost:	None

*E*stablishing a standard bedtime for children and sticking with it seems like a simple thing that's not really important. Until you realize it really isn't fun to have three kids jumping on the couch giggling at 11:00 the night before you have that big presentation at work. Sleep is good for both children and parents. An ever increasing problem observed by elementary school teachers is the number of children who come to school sleepy and even irritable for lack of sleep. Recent scientific studies also show that sleep, and the dreaming that occurs only during uninterrupted sleep, is directly linked to learning and remembering "how-to" skills. And a traditional and extremely reliable torture method used throughout the ages is sleep deprivation. But you knew that!

As a responsible parent, you probably keep your child indoors or at least supervised after dark, but there are several cultural trends that work against a parent's desire or even awareness that a standard bedtime policy needs to actually be established in every home. I will categorize these trends as "physical," "telecommunicable," and "emotional."

The physical trend is witnessed by the fact that many children simply do not want to go to sleep at night. Why is this? One of the primary reasons is because the children have not exhausted themselves into sleepiness. The answer: Get your kids out doing something physical. If you exercise for your health or enjoyment, have your kids go with you. There are all kinds of ways to get your kid his or her exercise, but you need to do it. This can help counteract the physical trend opposing a standard bedtime for your kids.

The "telecommunicable" trend affects people of all ages. It is witnessed by an array of television, video players, and other entertainment devices placed conveniently throughout the home. I facetiously call it communicable because it is like a disease. A disease that does not run its course and go away, but a disease like alcoholism that can only be overcome via intense personal desire and commitment (or a long-term power failure). Television is entertaining, often soothing, and sometimes hypnotic for both parent and child. The "best" shows are shown beginning at 8 o'clock and running on until 10 or 11 o'clock. The temptation to let kids stay up and watch their favorite shows is great, since they tend to be quieter that way and we as parents will have a short term respite if we give in to the child's desire, which allows us to watch the shows we want to watch. Here's what you can do:

∞ Pull the plug on the main TV at the bedtime hour. Eliminate televisions in the bedroom of any child who is under the age of eighteen.

∞ Establish a series of nighttime events that start at least thirty minutes before bedtime, and do not include the TV. This can include reading books, bathing, cleaning up the kitchen, eating a snack, looking at stars, taking a walk around the block together, you name it.

∞ Allow quiet bedroom activities like reading, puzzles, simple crafts, or sketching for a limited time before bedtime, especially for older kids. Use a kitchen timer to be be sure things don't get out of control.

∞ Skip the gimmicks, and simply make the kids go to bed. If your kids are used to gimmicks, and prefer them, this should not be attempted by the parent unless he or she has had a good day and feels energized at eight o'clock at night. On the other hand, if the parent feels lousy and has had a bad day, this may be the most expedient route.

The third cultural trend that works against established bedtimes for children is emotional. Our society has grown from viewing children as property to one that values children's rights. We, as a society, have fewer children, work more outside the home, and up to half of us either bear children or raise them without a resident spouse. This concentrates our sense of parenthood emotionally, and in many cases we think we need our children's approval as much as we know they need ours. Because of this, we may allow our children to stay up late at night frequently not just to avoid an argument, but because we really want to spend social time with them. The solution is to do social activities before the established bedtimes. This means cooking dinner together, and perhaps cleaning and doing housework after the children's bedtime. It means spending more of our limited time on social activities involving the children and less time on non-social activities. This goes for pre-teens and teens as much as for younger kids. Eliminate the parental guilt by doing the best you can, and believing that a standard workable bedtime for your kids is one of the valuable things you provide as a parent for your kid's benefit.

When establishing a standard bedtime, decide on a time that is age appropriate. Get the children's ideas and then give the whole exercise (if it is a change from the family's habits) a few weeks to become the new habit. Stick to it, and you'll find enormous benefits for your kids and for yourselves. References that can help include:

The Crying Baby by Sheila Kitzinger (Viking Penguin, 1989)

Helping Your Child Sleep Through the Night by Joanne Cuthbertson and Suzanne Schevill (Doubleday, 1985)

Solve Your Child's Sleep Problems by Richard Ferber (S&S Trade, 1986)

Nighttime Parenting: How to Get Your Baby and Child to Sleep by William Sears (La Leche League, 1985)

Other:

Baby-Go-To-Sleep Center   (Provides audio therapy tapes for
P. O. Box 1332   babies and children.)
Florence, AL 35631
1-800-537-7748

8. Create Space & Time To Dream

Time Cost:	None
Resource Cost:	None

Kids of all ages need space and time to think and absorb the world. A child's bedroom can be his or her own personal space, or a treehouse or doghouse or junk closet, or basement or porch. We adults often get this luxury when we drive our car, or go jogging or for walks. The space itself is somewhat important, and as parents we should look for opportunities where we live to ensure our child has access and even ownership of some personal space for imagining.

Even more important is time. If we are parents of the nineties, we probably are busy and expect and want our kids to be busy. We are competitive and expect our kids to be competitive. As we drive ourselves into burnout, we have the potential to drive our kids into burnout. For us, burnout can be overcome by rest, and short term change in our behavior. For our kids, burnout can result in a whole rejection of the strictures and high expectations of the parents, and can effect a sense of failure in the child. Check your kid's schedule, including time spent in transportation. Consider how much leisure time your kid really has to himself or herself. Even more importantly, how much control does your child have over his or her schedule? As adults, we know one of the biggest sources of stress on the job is having no sense of control over our jobs, our work, the quality of our product, or our assignments. Think about it.

If we think of stress, its causes, and its relation to how kids approach their lives and their problems, we can focus on doing simple things that can make a difference. Things that enable our kids, as in Munro Leaf's book, *The Story of Ferdinand*, "to sit just quietly and smell the flowers." We might learn something useful as well. Ask yourself the following questions:

∞ Does my child have a place he or she can go to get away from it all?

∞ Is my child frequently and routinely rushed by me and/or other people to be somewhere?

∞ Does my child complain of not having time to work on a favorite project, read a book, do homework, have fun, etc.?

∞ Is my child frequently afflicted with the "whine" syndrome? You'll know the answer to this question if you are frequently saying, "Stop that whining!"

The answer is to reduce stress by increasing the control that kids have over their environment. This means "a room of one's own" and free time. The room question should be worked out with parental leadership, in most cases. As far as "free time" goes— many adults think that time is limited and that there is never enough of it to go around. This is, of course, a fallacy. There is plenty of time to do everything that we want to do. The key is to define what we want to do and then establish the amount of time we are willing to spend on these efforts. Free time is created by prioritizing tasks and by being organized.

A few simple tips to create time for daydreaming, wandering, and wondering are provided below:

∞ Prepare for routine, recurring events, like mornings. Establish a routine, identify known tasks, and share the workload and responsibility among the whole family.

∞ Stop losing things! I actually don't believe in the word "lost." Most of what passes for lost is simply forgotten, and it is forgotten because it was misplaced. It was misplaced because there wasn't a convenient routine to be followed. Searching for lost items is a real time-waster. Spend a Saturday morning and put hooks up everywhere for things like keys, umbrellas, mittens; Make sure there is a standard place for items like bookbags, briefcases, pens, hairbrushes, hats, everything you routinely need.

∞ Plan for occasional events, instead of reacting. Keep a calendar of some kind in the kitchen to keep track of school and sporting events. If the calendar gets too congested because of all the things you and your family are signed up for, consider it a sign. Heed the sign by pulling back and reducing outside commitments and activities.

∞ Choose carefully the things you want to spend time on. Shopping for clothes and the home, attending social functions, cleaning the house, everything we do may need to be re-examined and re-prioritized. Do the same for your kids. Start by simply keeping a diary (or have your older kids do it for themselves) of your kids (and your own) daily schedule over a week's time. Simply knowing what you spend time on will give you and your kids a sense of control that reduces stress and ultimately creates free time.

∞ Stop promoting the illusion that everyone has to be busy all of the time. I remember one lazy weekend with relatives a long time ago: We were all sitting, resting, or dozing in the living room, no one talking, each lost in their own thoughts. Then we heard someone, one of the mothers, bustling around in the kitchen. Everyone looked up, and then at each other.

Someone commented,"I wonder if she's trying to make us feel guilty for not doing anything constructive?" My uncle commented, "Well, at least one person is working... that's good enough for me" and went back to doing nothing. We sometimes need to take the long view — as long as somebody is doing something "constructive" somewhere in the world, it's O.K. to take time for yourself.

For more information on de-stressing your life and your kid's life, as well as increasing free time, look to the following:

Busy Bodies: How We Become More Harried Even as We Become More Affluent by Lee Burns (Norton, 1993)

Time and the Art of Living by Robert Grudin (Ticknor and Fields, 1988)

Growing Up Creative: Nurturing a Lifetime of Creativity by Teresa Amabile (Creative Education Foundation, 1992)

Teaching Creative Behavior by Doris Shallcross (Bearly Ltd, 1985)

School's Out: Now What? Afternoon, Weekends, Vacation, Creative Choices for Your Child by Joan M. Bergstrom (Berkeley 10 Speed Press, 1990)

Stress Busters for Kids: A Parent's Guide to Helping Kids Cope with Stress by Bonnie M. Brown (B.M. Brown, 1990)

Organization:

The American Institute of Stress
124 Oark Avenue, Dept. B
Yonkers, NY 10703

The Hardiness Institute
19742 MacArthur Blvd., Suite 100
Irvine, CA 92715-2408

SECTION TWO

LEARNING AT HOME

This section describes how you can, with minimal expense of time or money, convert your child's living environment into a truly enhanced learning environment. The fifteen areas covered here contain a lot of ideas, most of which are easy and simple. Once you get started, you'll begin to see learning opportunities everywhere — and if you're not careful, you'll probably have fun, too!

1. Keep Craft & Creative Supplies Handy

Time Cost:	10 minutes a week
Resource Cost:	$0 to $50 annually

Your home with children should be replete with all kinds of items for crafts and art and construction. A large box, a bookshelf, or a filing cabinet should be set aside solely for the purpose of supplying your children with the raw materials to use in creating, crafting, and constructing. A partial list below is the minimum that should be available to your children — and I recommend that these purchases (where purchases are required) be taken from the Barbie, Ken, and matchbox car fund.

Colored pencils	Butcher paper
Crayons	Plain and lined paper
Charcoal pencils	Scissors
Sharpeners	Stapler
Glue (bottle & sticks)	Fabric scraps

Drinking straws	Cotton balls
Cardboard (pieces & boxes)	Brown paper grocery bags
Rulers and stencils	Toilet paper & paper towel rolls
Rubber bands	Chalk
Tape	Clay or modeling materials
Beads, old spools	Plaster of Paris
Old costume jewelry	Various kinds of pasta
String, yarn, and thread	Plastic lids
Interesting containers	Old candles and crayons
Egg cartons	Baby food jars
Cardboard inserts	Old magazines

Paints (watercolor and other non-toxic paints)
Paintbrushes (including old makeup brushes, toothbrushes, etc.)
Colored paper (construction, origami, and old wrapping paper)

Free art and learning supplies may be found locally. Likely sources include:

Possible Source	Type of Item/Supply
Home Decorating Stores	Outdated wallpaper books (for wrapping paper, decorating displays, designing stationery) Outdated carpet samples (making patchwork carpets, art creations)
Cabinet Shops and Furniture Factories	Small wood scraps (wood carving, art, and craft items)
Upholstery Shops	Outdated fabric samples and foam (art creations, bulletin boards, and craft items)
Newspaper Offices	End rolls of newsprint (murals, body tracings, bulletin board displays)

Books with more information and ideas include:

Recipes for Art and Craft Materials, Revised Edition by Helen R. Sattler (Lothrop, 1987)

Things That Kids Can Make: Easy Crafts for All Seasons by Nancy B. Anderson (Mark Inc, CA, 1992)

Incredibly Awesome Crafts for Kids by Better Homes and Gardens Staff (Meredith Books, 1992)

Look What I Made: Forty Craft Ideas and 120 Related Activities for Children Ages 2-5 by Joan W. Buma (Prima Publications, 1991)

Fifty Nifty Crafts to Make With Things Around the House by Cambria Cohen (Lowell House, 1992)

Crafts for Kids: A Month-to-Month Idea Book, Second Edition by Barbara L. Dandiego (TAB Books, 1990)

137 Crafts for Kids by Vanessa-Ann Collection Staff (Meredith Books, 1993)

Great Newspaper Crafts by F. Virginia Walter (Sterling, 1993)

Fun to Make Nature Crafts by Judith Conaway (Troll Associates, 1981)

132 Gift Crafts Kids Can Make, Grades 1-6 by Highlights Editors (Highlights, 1981)

128 Holiday Crafts Kids Can Make, Grades 1-6 by Highlights Editors (Highlights, 1981)

127 Anytime Crafts Kids Can Make, Grade 1-6 by Highlights Editors (Highlights, 1981)

What Can I Do Today? A Treasury of Crafts for Children by Joan F. Klimo (Pantheon, 1974)

The Never-Be-Bored Book: Quick Things to Make When There's Nothing to Do by Judith L. Lehne (Sterling, 1992)

"Dough-it-Yourself Handbook", 32 page book of decorating, craft and rainy-day projects for kids. Send $1.00 to Morton Salt Consumer Affairs, Dept 1137, 100 N. Riverside Plaza, Chicago, IL 60606-1597

Some sources for craft supplies include the following:

Boycan's Craft Supplies
P.O. Box 897
Sharon, PA 16146

Chaselle
9645 Gerwig Lane
Columbia, MD 21046

Craftsman Corporation
4118 Lakeside Drive
Richmond, CA 94806
(415) 223-3144

The Craft Basket
Hoover Road
Stevens Point, WI 54481

Craft King
P.O. Box 90637
Lakeland, FL 33804
(813) 686-9600

Craft Service
337 University Avenue
Rochester, NY 14607
(716) 325-5547

Creative Crafts
16 Plains Road
P.O. Box 819
Essex, CT. 06426.

Dick Blick Arts and Crafts
P.O. Box 1267
Galesburg, IL 61401.

Enterprise Art
Dept 681
P.O. Box 2918
Largo, FL 34649
(813) 536-1492

Florida Supply House Catalog
P.O. Box 847
Bradenton, FL 33506

House of Crafts & Stuff, Inc
5157 Gall Blvd, Highway 301
Zephyrhills, FL 33541
(813) 782-0223

J & A Crafts
210 Front Street
Hempstead, NY 11550

Kelly's Crafts, Inc
P.O. Box 219
Ross, OH 45061
1-800-828-9818

Pearl Paint Company
308 Canal Street
New York, NY 10013
1-800-221-6845

**Suncoast Discount
Craft Supplies**
9015 U.S. Highway 19 N
Pinellas Park, FL 34666
(813) 577-6331

Zeigler Art-Craft Supply
P.O. Box 50037
Tulsa, OK 74150
(918) 584-2217

Minnesota Clay Company
8001 Grand Avenue
Bloomington, MN 55420
(612) 884-9101

S & S Arts and Crafts
Norwich Avenue
Colchester, CT 06415

Vanguard Arts & Crafts Supplies
1081 East 48 Street
Brooklyn, NY 11234
1-800-662-7238

2. Art Everywhere!

Time Cost:	None
Resource Cost:	Zero to $200 a year

When a child's interest relates to the arts, we should say, not "No!" but "Why not?" Children are capable of creating and appreciating art and beauty — sometimes more openly and perceptively than we adults. We need to encourage these sensitivities in every way we can, and luckily, it's not difficult.

This doesn't mean attempting to create artistic geniuses via intense one-on-one tutoring by a grand master. It does mean looking for and sometimes creating opportunities to add to your child's perspectives and fostering his or her sense of ability and appreciation for art. One of the most important aspects is timing. Your child learns more from your attitude towards his or her latest interest than he or she will learn from your personal knowledge of the subject. To communicate the importance of the child's interest, the key ingredient is not what you do, but when and how you do it. Here are some ideas to try:

∞ Encourage your children to notice the art around them. Keep magazines around for cutting out pictures and photos of interest. Make sure there is a place to post these pictures. Ask your child why they like a particular picture or painting, or why they don't like it.

∞ Keep and post your child's creations. One thing that really communicates the artistic value of children's drawings and paintings is to frame them (not at a frame shop, but simply placing the artwork in an inexpensive metal or wooden frame). Keep several of these frames around in various sizes, just for this purpose. Put them up on the walls throughout the house. The picture that seems average and childish, when framed on the wall, suddenly becomes an artistic decoration anywhere you place it.

∞ On your way home from work, pick up library books or check out magazines that focus on your child's latest interest, whether it is art, music, or anything else.

∞ Videos on the subject of interest can also be checked out, free at libraries, and at low cost in video stores.

∞ Find (or ask community centers or local schools to offer) art, drama, clay, sculpture, tap, ballet or music classes for children. Take advantage of these opportunities while your children are young.

∞ Encourage your children to take photos, using old or inexpensive cameras. Experiment with black and white film or color. Give film as gifts for birthdays and special occasions.

∞ Give art (prints of famous artists from Monet to Picasso to pop art to Grandma Moses) to your children for birthdays, holidays, and other occasions. Keep a can of spackle around to remind yourself that holes really can be made in your walls, whether you own or rent.

∞ Take your family to art museums, shows, and craft fairs. Frequent yard sales and flea markets with an eye to low-cost art. The idea with young children is not investment quality art, but rather variety and exposure to the many kinds of beauty around us.

∞ Get your children interested in going to local libraries. Help them get their own library cards. Show them where the art books are, in both the juvenile and the adult sections.

∞ Go with your children to locally produced plays and presentations. Encourage your children to get involved in theatric events at school, day-care, within the community, and at-home, if they seem interested.

For more information, see the following:

Books and Pamphlets:

Understanding and Appreciating Your Child's Art: How to Enhance Confidence in Drawing, Ages 2-12 by Mia Johnson (Lowell House, 1992)

Diamonds in the Dust: Discover and Develop Your Child's Gifts by Jackie Mallis (MultiMedia, TX, 1992)

Children are Artists: An Introduction to Children's Art for Teachers and Parents (Stanford University Press, 1989)

Art Projects for Young Children by Jane A. Caballero (Humanics Ltd., 1978)

Making Models: Three-D Creations from Paper and Clay by Diana Craig (Millbrook Press, 1993)

Arts and Crafts from Things Around the House by Imogene Forte (Incentive Publications, 1983)

"Children & Parents & Arts." Five pamphlets totaling 25 pages with creative ideas to help children develop their artistic skills in theater, writing, music, dance, and the visual arts. Send 50 cents to the Consumer Information Center-2D, P.O. Box 100, Pueblo, CO 81002.

"Tips to Make Your Kids Art Smart" Send a self-addressed stamped, business-size envelope to Art Ventures International, 1001 Fifth Avenue, New York, N. Y. 10028.

Organizations:

National Art Education Association
1916 Association Drive
Reston, VA 22091

Theatreworks/USA
890 Broadway
New York, NY 10003

Children's Art Foundation
915 Cedar Street
Santa Cruz, CA 95060

Sources:

Decor Prints
Box 502
Noel, MO 64854

The University Prints
Box 485
Winchester, MA 01890

Art Reproduction Catalog
The Museum of Fine Arts
P.O. Box 1044
Boston, MA 02120

Art Poster Company
29555 Northwestern Highway, Ste 234
Southfield, MI 48034

Gallery of Prehistoric Paintings
25-60 49th Street 2nd Floor
Astoria, NY 11103

Periodicals:

KidsArt News (quarterly)
912 Schilling Way
Mount Shasta, CA 96067

Arts in Residence (monthly)
235 Pasadena
Tustin, CA 92680

3. Maps

Time Cost:	10 minutes a week
Resource Cost:	$0 - $100

*E*very home with kids needs to have at least one globe, and as many maps as possible. World maps, United States maps, state, county and city maps should be available. Globes should be out where kids can spin them, and they should be encouraged to do so. Maps should be posted at the eye level of the children in the home, and in rooms that the family uses so they can be referenced in discussion of other things. When the TV news comes on, countries and cities in the news should be pointed out on the maps for and by the children. Events of interest reported in the newspaper should also be located on the maps. There are many games that can be played that result in locating and naming capitals, historical sites, and sources of strange products, and posted maps facilitate this.

Road maps should be available to not just the driver in the family, but the whole family. Treks to grandmother's house and vacations, can be marked on maps for even the youngest children to view. Maps and globes are inexpensive ways to ensure your child is aware of the great big world, and to some extent his or her ability to master it.

For sources of maps and globes, local Chambers of Commerce, for local and regional maps, travel maps and historical points of interest maps. State Offices of Tourism offer great state maps, with historical and unique locations annotated and described.

Other sources of maps and information include:

"Helping Your Child Learn Geography" A 33 page booklet designed to teach children geography in a style that is challenging and fun. Send fifty cents to the Consumer Information Center-2D, P.O. Box 100, Pueblo, CO 81002

US Department of the Interior
US Geological Survey
900 National Center
Reston, VA 22092

National Geographic Society
P.O. Box 2895
Washington, D.C. 20077-9960
1-800-447-0647

American Geographic Society
Suite 1501, 25 West 39th Street
New York, NY 10018

American Map Corporation
46-35 54th Road
Maspeth, NY 11378

ABC School Supply
6500 Peachtree Industrial Blvd
P.O. Box 4750
Norcross, GA 30091
(404) 447-5000

Creative Imaginations, Inc
(714) 995-2266

Geolearning Corporation
Sheridan, WY 82801

World Image
Suite 104-GT
6348 West 95th Street
Oak Lawn, IL 60453
(708) 233-0208

Orienteering Services
P.O. Box 1604
Binghamton, NY 13902

Rand McNally
P.O. Box 7600
Chicago, IL 60680

4. Home As School

Time Cost:	30 to 60 minutes a week
Resource Cost:	$0 to $200 annually

he home schooling movement has been expanding rapidly, largely in response to what many feel is a lack of quality in public education. While most of us don't have the confidence or desire to home school our children, we can all learn from what home schoolers do. I'll summarize what they "do" in three ways:

1) Home schooling parents have confidence in their ability to teach their children;

2) Home schooling parents seek out expert assistance for curriculum development and learning tools, and;

3) Home schooling parents improvise to turn everyday situations into learning opportunities.

To me, that doesn't sound radical. It sounds like what we should all be doing for our children. To get started, we must first accept that we <u>can</u> teach our children. If we do nothing at all in the next twenty years, we will still teach our children an incredible amount of what they will learn in those twenty years. The key thing we want to accomplish is to turn the home and community into a learning laboratory for our children.

For more information on what you can do:

Books:

How to Be a Gifted Parent by David Lewis (Berkley, 1982)

Awakening Your Child's Natural Genius: Enhancing Your Child's Natural Curiosity, Creativity and Learning Ability by Thomas Armstrong (J. P. Tarcher, 1991)

Parents Are Teachers Too: Enriching Your Child's First Six Years by Claudia Jones (Williamson Publishing Company, 1988)

You Can Teach Your Child Successfully: Grades Four through Eight by Ruth Beechick (Arrow Press, 1992)

Teach Your Own by John Holt (Delacorte, 1982)

A Home Start in Reading by Ruth Beechick (Arrow Press, 1985)

Slow and Steady, Get Me Ready: A How-to Book That Grows with the Child by June R. Oberlander (Bio-Alpha, 1992)

Taking Charge Through Home Schooling: Personal and Political Empowerment by Larry M. Kaseman and Susan D. Kaseman (Koshkonong Press, 1991)

Home Schooling: Answering Questions by K. Williamson (C.C. Thomas, 1989)

Home School Sourcebook by Donn Reed (Brook Farm Books, 1991)

An Easy Start in Arithmetic: Grades K-3 by Ruth Beechick (Arrow Press, 1986)

Family Math, published by the "Family Math Program," Lawrence Hall of Science, University of California, Berkeley, CA 94720, phone (510) 642-1823. Features hands-on math learning at home.

Home Education Resource Guide, available from Blue Bird Publishing, 1713 E. Broadway, Suite 306, Tempe, AZ 85282, 1-800-654-1993 or (602) 968-4088

"You Can Help Your Child Learn Mathematics" An 8 page booklet with fun ideas to help young school age children connect their real-life experiences with the math they need to learn. Write to: Consumer Information Center-2D, P.O. Box 100, Pueblo, CO 81002.

"Home Team Learning Activities" A free brochure containing many tips on helping kids learn at home. Write to: American Federation of Teachers, Dept P. P.O. Box 2090, Washington, D.C. 20013-2090.

Organizations:

Center for Home Schooling
P.O. Box 250
Amherst, N.H. 03031
(603) 882-8688

Home Education Press
P.O. Box 1083
Tonasket, WA 98855
(509) 486-1351

Oak Meadow
P.O. Box 712
Blacksburg, VA 24060
(703) 552-3263

(Offers home curriculum that can be used as a supplement to regular school.)

National Home School Association
P.O. Box 157290
Cincinnati, OH 45215-7290
(513) 772-9580

Holt Associates
2269 Massachusetts Avenue
Boston, MA 02140
(617) 864-3100

Suppliers of school supplies, furniture, and science kits include:

ABC School Supply
6500 Peachtree Industrial Blvd
P.O. Box 4750
Norcross, GA 30091
(404) 447-5000

Childcraft
20 Kilmore Road
Edison, NJ 08837
(201) 572-6100
1-800-631-5652

Educators Publishing Service, Inc
75 Moulton Street
Cambridge, MA 02138-1104

Educational Activities, Inc
P.O. Box 87
Baldwin, NY 11510
(516) 223-4666
1-800-645-3739

Chaselle
9645 Gerwig Lane
Columbia, MD 21046

Natural Science Industry, Ltd
Far Rockaway, NY 11691

Ideal School Supply
11000 S. Lavergne Avenue
Oak Lawn, IL 60453

Geolearning Corporation
Sheridan, WY 82801

Educational Materials Association
P.O. Box 7385
Charlottesville, VA 22906

Educational Teaching Aids
199 Carpenter Avenue
Wheeling, IL 60090
(312) 520-2500

Constructive Playthings
2008 W. 103 Road Ter.
Leawood, KS 66206
(816) 761-5900

Workman Publishing
708 Broadway
New York, NY 10003

Curiosity Kits - Adventures in Arts, Sciences and World Cultures
P.O. Box 811
Cockeysville, MD 21030

National Energy Foundation
5160 Wiley Post Way, Suite 200
Salt Lake City, UT 84116
(801) 539-1406

Didax Educational Resources
395 Main Street
Rowley, MA 01969
(508) 948-2340

Earth Science/Life Science Hubbard Scientific
P.O. Box 760
Chippewa Falls, WI 54729-0760
(312) 272-7810

Heathkit Educational Systems
Heath Company
P.O. Box 1288
Benton Harbor, MI 49023
(616) 925-6000
1-800-444-3284

Good Apple
P.O. Box 299
Carthage, IL 62321
(217) 357-3981
1-800-435-7234

F.D. Enterprises, Inc
P.O. Box 1751
Rockville, MD 20849

Sensational Beginnings
300 Detroit Ave #E
P.O. Box 2009
Monroe, MI 48161
1-800-444-2147

Edmund Scientific
101 E. Gloucester Pike
Barrington, N.J. 08007-1380
1-800-458-0024

Educational Insights, Inc
19560 S. Rancho Way
Dominguez Hills, CA 90220
(310) 637-2131
1-800-933-3277

J.L. Hammett Company
30 Hammett Place
Braintree , MA 02184
(617) 848-1000

Opportunities for Learning, Inc.
20417 Nordoff Street
Chatsworth, CA 91311
(818) 341-2535

Hearthsong
6519 N. Galena Road
P.O. Box 1773
Peoria, IL 61656-1773
(309) 689-3838
1-800-325-2502

Matthew Bender and Company
P.O. Box 989
Albany, NY 12201
(518) 462-6445

Southeastern Fossil Supply Company
1209 N. Eastman Road, Ste J209
Kingsport, TN 37664
(615) 245-3704

Troll Learn & Play
100 Corporate Drive
Mahwah, N.J. 07430
(201) 529-4000
1-800-247-6106

Puzzles and Such, Inc.
P.O. Box 3118
Hutchinson, KS 67504

The Learning Works
P.O. Box 6187
Santa Barbara, CA 93160

5. Science & Discovery

Time Cost:	30 to 60 minutes a week
Resource Cost:	$0 to $200 annually

Your home can be a scientific mystery, and you should aspire to this goal! Our immediate environment contains the wonders of the world, if we only look and see. To help your child look, see, and touch the science all around us doesn't take a lot of time or a lot of money. You should set up an environment for your children that encourages experimentation. With kids, it doesn't take much to encourage scientific experimentation — and likewise, it doesn't take much more than a bad attitude to discourage it. Some ideas to try are listed below:

∞ Create your own in-house science center. Every home should have a place where it is OK to have jars of bugs, milk cartons with seeds and plants growing in them, and a place to break open shells and crush rocks. A place to put a leftover lunch to watch it mold and decompose. Someplace in the house or backyard for large pets, if possible, as well as small pets like fish, turtles, rabbits, guinea pigs and spiders.

∞ For a child suddenly interested in a certain type of animal because of a book read, a picture noticed, or a television show, arrange trips to the zoo, farm or pet store. If the interest is in plants, geology, the ocean, or weather, visits to science museums, weather stations, and aquariums should be arranged.

∞ Find someone in your neighborhood who knows something about the subject matter your child is interested in, and make contact with them. Look for volunteer or paid tutors or instructors from the local retired community, community center, or schools and community colleges.

∞ Some science activities (especially when children "have nothing to do") include the following:

• Make a circle with string (about 4-8 feet long) in the back yard, and have each child collect a sample of everything that is growing within that enclosed area.

• Take a sheet of clear plastic wrap or cheesecloth, and place it over a part of your backyard. Put weights (rocks or dirt) around the edges, and wait one hour. Collect as many bugs as you can when you return. Identify them if you can.

• Go on a nature walk, bringing along several plastic bags, jars, and netting to collect samples. When you get home, categorize and display the items collected — by color (grey rocks, grey feathers, and grey twigs) or by texture (smooth to rough), by shape and size, by source (animal, vegetable, or mineral), or create a artistic collage by gluing items on a heavy posterboard, cardboard, or other flat surface. Or use the items in your terrarium, aquarium, or birdhouse.

• Make kites from plastic bags of various sizes, as well as plastic sheets, aluminum foil, paper and wooden or wire frames. See which work best.

• Make paper airplanes, gliders or boats. Experiment with different materials, including lightweight cardboard, wood, foils, and plastic. Fly and float them.

• Take every ball in the house and measure how high each one bounces when dropped from the same height. Then measure how far you can kick each ball. Measure the speed of each ball when it rolls downhill or down an inclined plane (a playground slide, for example).

• Bake bread, having the kids mix yeast, water, sugar or honey first, then mixing and kneading in flour, rising, and baking. You might even be able to eat it when you're done!

• Make homemade butter by filling a small clear jar half full with room-temperature heavy whipping cream, and shaking it. Pass the jar around so everyone gets a chance. Separate the buttermilk from the solidified butter, and spread fresh butter on bread or crackers. Compare this to purchased butter and margarine.

• With your children, collect trash or litter on the side of the road where you live, or in your yard, church, or some other relatively safe place. Categorize what you find and talk about why those items and not others are discarded as litter.

• Take flowers from the yard or garden, or celery stalks, and place them in water colored with food coloring. Observe what happens over time, then experiment with various types of plants, flowers, and colors.

• Take various shapes and sizes of glass bottles and jars, fill with various levels of water, and tap lightly with a spoon. Experiment with the sounds and try to play a song. Number the bottles, and write down the music so even a parent can play it.

For more information:

Books:

Science Everywhere: Opportunities for Very Young Children by Barbara J. Taylor (Harcourt Brace Jovanovich College Publishers, 1993)

Mr Wizard's Supermarket Science by Dan Herbert (Random House, 1980)

The Science Cookbook: Experiments That Teach Science and Nutrition by Julia B. Waxter (Fearon Teacher Aids, 1981)

Inventor's Workshop by Alan J. McCormack (Fearon Teacher Aids, 1981)

175 More Science Experiments to Amaze and Amuse Your Friends by Terry Cash, Steve Parker, and Barbara Taylor (Random House, 1990)

Backyard Science Series by Jane Hoffman (Backyard Scientist, 1989) (Write to Backyard Scientist, P.O. Box 16966, Irvine, CA 92713)

Sharing Nature with Children by Joseph Cornell (Dawn CA, 1979)

Sharing the Joy of Nature: Nature Activities for All Children by Joseph Cornell (Dawn CA, 1989)

Fabulous Paper Airplanes by Richard E. Churchill (Sterling, 1991)

Paper Science Toys by Richard E. Churchill (Sterling, 1990)

Exploring Fields and Lots: Easy Science Projects by Seymour Simon (Garrard, 1978)

Organizations and Sources:

National Science Teachers Association (NSTA)
1742 Connecticut Avenue, NW
Washington, DC 20009
(202) 328-5800

Earth Science/Life Science Hubbard Scientific
P.O. Box 760
Chippewa Falls, WI 54729-0760
(312) 272-7810

Teacher's Laboratory, Inc
P.O. Box 6480
Brattleboro, VT 05302
(802) 254-3457

Insect Lore Products
P.O. Box 1535
Shafter, CA 93263

National Audobon Society
950 Third Avenue
New York, NY 10022

**Conservation Foundation
"Aids to Educators"**
1717 Massachusetts Avenue, NW
Washington, D.C. 20036

INVENT America!
510 King Street, Suite 420
Alexandria, VA 22314

Kids for Saving the Earth
P.O. Box 47247
Plymouth, MA 55447-0247

Safari, Ltd
P.O. Box 630685
Miami, FL 33163

Natural Science Industry, Ltd
Far Rockaway, NY 11691

Constructive Playthings
2008 W. 103 Road Ter.
Leawood, KS 66206
(816) 761-5900

**Cuisenaire Material for
Learning, Mathematic
& Science, Cuisenaire
Company of America**
12 Church Street, Box D
New Rochelle, NY 10802
(914) 235-0900

**Curiosity Kits - Adventures
in Arts, Sciences &
World Cultures**
P.O. Box 811
Cockeysville, MD 21030

National Energy Foundation
5160 Wiley Post Way, Suite 200
Salt Lake City, UT 84116
(801) 539-1406

6. Encourage Collections & Collecting

Time Cost:	5 minutes a week
Resource Cost:	$0 - $50 annually

In your home, there should be a place for your child to keep and display his or her collections, of all kinds. Collecting and maintaining collections teaches your child the following, all painlessly and naturally:

> ∞ Attention to detail
> ∞ Classification and organization
> ∞ Research
> ∞ Pride that comes from adding and discovering value where none was seen before.

Collection ideas include:

- Rocks and minerals
- Baseball and sports cards
- Fossils
- Trading cards, any kind

- Small china animals
- Matchboxes/covers
- Patches
- Stamps
- Leaves
- Insects
- Matchbox cars
- Seashells
- Cans
- Gum wrappers
- Teddy bears
- Banana and fruit stickers
- Autographs
- Figurines
- Bottlecaps
- Postcards
- Coins
- Comic books
- Ticket stubs
- Dolls
- Seeds and seedpods
- Bottles
- Sand and soil
- Books
- Political memorabilia
- Cans
- Water from oceans, lakes, and rivers

Once your child has a collection, of any kind, take care to show it to visitors in your home, and take it to your child's school for show and tell, or sharing. Make a point to assist your child by simply being aware of what he or she is collecting at the moment, and bring home books, information, or samples from your daily rounds when you can.

For information on collections of the more popular types, write to or call the following:

Coins:

Amerian Numismatic Association
818 N. Cascade Avenue
Colorado Springs, CO 80903-3279
(719) 632-2646 or 1-800-367-9723

Numismatics International
P.O. Box 670013
Dallas, TX 75367
(214) 361-7543

Rocks, Minerals, and Fossils:

American Federation of Mineralogical Societies (AFMS)
920 SW 70th Street
Oklahoma City, OK 73193
(405) 631-2674

Mineralogical Society of America
1625 I Street NW Suite 414
Washington, D.C. 2006
(202) 775-4344

The Treasure Chest
Rt 40 Box 54
Havre de Grace, MD 21078
(301) 939-4468

Illustrated Fossil Catalog
J.F. Ray
P.O. Box 1364, Dept H
Ocala, FL 32678

Miners
P.O. Box 1301
Riggins, ID 83549

Earth Science/Life Science
Hubbard Scientific
P.O. Box 760
Chippewa Falls, WI 54729-0760
(312) 272-7810

Southeastern Fossil Supply
Company
1209 N. Eastman Road, Ste J209
Kingsport, TN 37664
(615) 245-3704

Postcards:

Autographs

Barr's Postcard News
70 S. Sixth Street
Lansing, IA 52151

The Autograph Collectors
Magazine
P.O. Box 55328
Stockton, CA 95205

Stamps:

Junior Philatelists of America
P.O. Box 701010
San Antonio, TX 78270
(210) 650-0507

Benjamin Franklin Junior
Stamp Club
U.S Postal Service
475 L'Enfant Plaza, Room 5630
Washington, D.C. 20260
(202) 268-2352

Political:

American Political Items Collectors
Box 340339
San Antonio, TX 78234

Baseball/Sports Cards:

Baseball Card News
700 E. State Street
Iola, WI 54990
(715) 445-2214

Baseball Card Digest
22203 John R. Road
Hazel Park, MI 48030

Insects:

**Young Entomologist's
Society, Inc**
151 Natural Science Building
Michigan State University
Lansing, MI 48910-2553
(517) 353-9386

Seashells:

**American Malacological
Union**
3706 Rice Blvd
Houston, TX 77005
(713) 668-8752

Sand:

**International Sand Collector's
Society**
43 Highview Avenue
Old Greenwich, CT 06870
(203) 637-2801

7. Give Your Child A Magazine Subscription

Time Cost:	10 minutes a year
Resource Cost:	$0 - $50 annually

Your children need to be aware of the world outside them and feel connected to it. They also need to feel special. A great way to do both, relatively inexpensively, is to allow them to subscribe to their own magazine, based on their interests. Some youth magazines are listed below, for starters:

"Highlights" for Children, ages 2 to 12, eleven issues per year. Features "fun with a purpose." Write to Highlights for Children, P.O. Box 182051, Columbus, OH 43218-2051

"Ladybug," ages 2-7, monthly. Write to Ladybug, Carcis Publications, 315 Fifth Street, Peru, IL 61354

"Sesame Street Magazine," ages 2-6, ten issues per year. Filled with Sesame Street characters, magazine introduces basic skills.

Write to Sesame Street Magazine, P.O. Box 55518, Boulder, CO 80322-5518

"Your Big Backyard," ages 3-5, ten issues per year. Published by the National Wildlife Federation. Write to Your Big Backyard, National Wildlife Federation, 8925 Leesburg Pike, Vienna, VA 22184-0001

"Chickadee," ages 3-9, monthly. Puzzles, stories, poems and photos based on a nature theme. Write to Chickadee, Young Naturalist Foundation, 56 The Esplanade, Suite 306, Toronto, Ontario, M5E 1A7 Canada or to P.O. Box 11314, Des Moines, IA 50340

"Owl," grades 3-9. Monthly. Discovery magazine for children. Write to Owl, Young Naturalist Foundation, 56 The Esplanade, Suite 306, Toronto, Ontario, M5E 1A7 Canada or P.O. Box 11314, Des Moines, IA 50340

"Spark! : The Magazine of Creative Fun for Kids," ages 3-12. Write to Spark!, P.O. Box 5028, Harlan, IA 51593-2528

"KidCity," ages 6-9, monthly. General youth interests and activities. Children's Television Network, One Lincoln Plaza, New York, NY 10023

"Ranger Rick," ages 6-12, monthly. Published by the National Wildlife Federation. Write to Ranger Rick, National Wildlife Federation, 8925 Leesburg Pike, Vienna, VA 22184-0001

"Zoobooks," ages 6-14, ten issues per year. Published by Wildlife Education, Limited. Write to Zoobooks Wildlife Education, Limited, 3590 Kettner Blvd, San Diego, CA 92101

"Cricket: The Magazine for Children," ages 6-12, monthly. A literary magazine featuring stories and poems by well-known authors. Write to Cricket, Box 387, Mount Morris, IL 61054-0387 or to Carcis Publications, 315 Fifth Street, Peru, IL 61354

"Crayola Kids," ages 4-12, an arts and crafts activity magazine published by Better Homes and Gardens, P.O. Box 4536, Des Moines, IA 50336, or call 1-800-846-7968.

"Stone Soup: The Magazine for Children," ages 6-13, a children's literary magazine published five times a year. Write to Stone Soup, Children's Art Foundation, 915 Cedar Street, Santa Cruz, CA 95060

"National Geographic World," ages 8-13, monthly. Stories, facts, and games about wild animals, sports, pets, hobbies, and other kids. Write to National Geographic World, National Geographic Society, 17th and M Street, NW, Washington, D.C. 20036

"P3: The Earth-Based Magazine for Kids," ages 6-13, ten issues a year. Write to P3 Foundation, P.O. Box 52, Montgomery, VT 05470

"3-2-1 Contact!" ages 8-12, monthly. Science, nature and technology magazine for children. Write to 3-2-1 Contact, Children's Television Network, One Lincoln Plaza, New York, NY 10023

"New Moon: The Magazine for Girls," ages 7-16, Write to New Moon, P.O. Box 3587, Duluth, MN 55803-3587

"Boy's Life," ages 9-14, monthly. Published for those interested in Scouting. Write to Boy's Life, Boy Scouts of America, 1325 West Walnut Hill Lane, P.O. Box 152079, Irving, TX 75015-2079

"Penny Power," ages 8-14. bimonthly. Published by Consumer Reports, designed to create intelligent young consumers. Write to Penny Power, Subscription Department, Box 51777, Boulder, CO 80321

"Creative Kids," ages 8-14, elementary and middle school age. Forum for budding authors, illustrators, and photographers, publishing creative works by children. Write to Creative Kids, 350 Weinacker Avenue, P.O. Box 6448, Dept 1-I, Mobile, AL 36660-0448

"Odyssey," ages 8-14, monthly. Magazine about astronomy and outer space. Write to Odyssey, Kalmbach Publishing, 21027 Crossroads Circle, P.O. Box 1612, Waukesha, WI 53187-1612

"Cobblestone: The History Magazine for Young People," ages 8-14, ten issues per year. Write to Cobblestone, 30 Grove Street, Peterborough, NH 03458

"Faces: The Magazine About People," ages 8-14, 10 issues per year. An introduction to history and cultures around the world. Write to Faces, 30 Grove Street, Peterborough, NH 03458

"Calliope: World History for Young People," ages 8-14, 10 issues per year. An introduction to history and cultures around the world. Write to Calliope, 30 Grove Street, Peterborough, NH 03458

"Think, Inc," ages 8-12, monthly. Write to Think, Inc, P.O. Box 5275, Arvada, CO 80005

"Merlyn's Pen: The National Magazine of Student Writing," ages 12-18, quarterly. Stories and poems by students in grades 7 through 12. Write to Merlyn's Pen, P.O. Box 1058, East Greenwich, RI 02818

"Insect World," ages 6-15, bimonthly. Insect facts, stories, poems, insect lore, trivia, artwork, game and activity ideas, book and resource reviews. Write to Young Entomologist's Society, Inc, Education Department, 1915 Peggy Place, Lansing, MI 48910-2553

"The World of Business Kids," ages 10-19. Write to Business Kids/America's Future, Lemonade Kids, Inc, Suite 330, 301 Almeia Avenue, Coral Gables, FL 33134

"Sports Illustrated for Kids," ages 8-19, monthly. Write to Time-Warner, Time and Life Building, New York, NY 10020

8. Write

Time Cost:	10 minutes a week
Resource Cost:	$5 to $20 annually

In the age of electronic media, the art of writing — letters, compositions, poetry, stories and reports — is an art to be fully nurtured and cherished. Here's what you do:

∞ Make sure each child (and each parent) in the family has their own stash of stationery, pens, pencils and markers, and stamps, all easily available to them.

∞ Insist on thank you letters for all gifts and favors, visits and tours. Just do it, and make it a habit. If you have to bribe kids to write those letters with TV, treats, or favorite activities, I think it is worth it.

∞ Encourage your child to write away for information and catalogs. If they show an interest in something and want more answers than you have on hand, assist your child in getting right addresses.

∞ For children who are too young to write, have them draw pictures to send to relatives, and/or have them dictate to you what they would like to say and send this in a letter.

∞ Sign your child up for newsletters, birthday clubs, and put them on mailing lists from local colleges, community centers, or libraries, so he or she will get his own mail.

∞ Sign up for a penpal. This can be done through various children's penpal organizations, or through your child's classroom. Suggest to your child's teacher that he or she establish classroom pen pals in foreign countries, or adopt military or State Department personnel stationed in foreign countries.

∞ Encourage your children to write to the President, Vice-President, and members of Congress, as well as sports or entertainment celebrities. Write to the local newspaper, to comment or ask for more information on a particular story or news report. Write to authors or illustrators of favorite books, care of the book publisher.

∞ Write notes to your kids for their lunchboxes, bookbags, under their pillow, on the refrigerator, and encourage them to write notes back to you.

∞ Write a family cookbook together. Write out favorite recipes, and describe not only how to make it, but what makes it good and special. Let the kids lead the project, and keep it in a looseleaf notebook so you can add to it over time.

∞ Make sure each child has a notebook or journal. Encourage your child to frequently write down personal observations in their own journal, including pictures and drawings.

∞ Have your child or children help put together a holiday or birthday newsletter to send to friend and relatives.

∞ Have kids make their own greeting cards, valentine cards, and birthday cards to send to friends and relatives.

∞ Have children make their own signs and posters for their rooms and school functions. Have them make signs for your next garage sale, for your car, or office. Next time you place an ad in the newspaper, have your kids write and/or design it for you.

∞ Write poetry at home. Haiku, three lined poems with seven syllables in the first and last lines, and five syllables in the middle line, are fun and don't take a lot of time to get started. Haiku usually has nature as a subject matter. Another fun poetry is the limerick — five lines, the first two rhyming with the last, and lines three and four shorter and rhyming with each other.

∞ Make books together, using collections of poems (both favorites from books and magazines, and homegrown), sports activities, and records of trips and visits.

For more information, see the following books and pamphlets:

Families Writing by Peter Stillman (Writer's Digest Books, 1989)

The Art of Teaching Writing by Lucy McCormick Colkins (Heinemann, 1986)

Growing Up Writing by Linda L. Lamm (Acropolis, 1984)

Write Throughout the Year by Wanda Lincoln (Monday Morning Books, 1989)

Kids Have All the Write Stuff: Inspiring Your Child to Put Pencil to Paper by Sharon A. Edwards and Robert W. Maloy (Viking Penguin, 1992)

"Help Your Child Learn to Write Well." A five-page booklet with simple strategies for adults to help encourage children who are just learning to express their ideas through writing. Send fifty cents to the Consumer Information Center-2D, P.O. Box 100, Pueblo, CO 81002.

Organizations:

Young Writers Club
Box 216
Newburyport, MA 01950

National Council of Teachers of English
1111 Kenyon Road
Urbana, IL 61801

9. Play Games With Your Children

Time Cost:	45 minutes a week
Resource Cost:	$0 - $100

he problem with most games is that they take time — time we busy parents don't really believe we have. The good thing about them is that they are fun and the time passes quickly. The reason they are fun is because your kids are fun, and usually we don't see how fun they are because we don't sit down or go out with them long enough to find out. In addition to being fun, playing games in a family environment is a good way to develop in your children a sense of fair play, and an ability to lose and win gracefully. These skills are in fact <u>not</u> taught in school and are learned through parental example and through practice. I even have a theory that the ability to lose gracefully is perhaps the biggest part of self-esteem. A graceful loser (and winner) is one who understands that losing a game, losing social stature in the group, losing a position in life is normal and not the definer of the individual's personal worth. We should all aspire to this kind of grace. For all these reasons, try the following to get into the family game habit:

∞ Set aside an evening a week when everyone will be there to play a board game. Allow a window of time, perhaps forty-five minutes or an hour, for the game, and don't start too late in the evening. Keep the TV off.

∞ Get help clearing the kitchen table or coffee table, and have the kids set up everything for your game. They'll probably be slightly more motivated than you to set up the game, so have them call you when it's ready.

∞ Have some healthy snacks available so game night can also be a snack night.

∞ Pick a game that is appropriate for your age group. Don't go directly by the age groups listed on the game box. If you have children of varying ages, just figure out handicaps for some and credits for others so that the game can be played by the whole family.

NOTE: Purists may not accept my laissez faire approach to game rules, but I think building enjoyment through participation is more effective than through passive viewing. The skills and understanding of the rules will develop over time, and meanwhile you've had the pleasure of your children's company.

∞ Don't forget two-person games like chess, checkers, and backgammon. In fact, on game night, your family can break up into groups for these games, if the ages and interests work out that way.

∞ Buy games at yard sales, or at the end-of-summer sales. A well-stocked garage or game shelf should have the following:

Outdoor Activities

- Bats and softballs/baseballs
- Basketball
- Croquet set
- Tennis balls

- Soccer ball
- Jump ropes
- Chalk (for marking)

- Frisbees
- Hula hoops
- Volleyball with net

Indoor Activities

- Checkers
- Scrabble
- Parcheesi
- Marbles

- Chess
- Monopoly
- Backgammon
- Trivia games

Books to look for include:

The Cooperative Sports and Games Book: Challenge Without Competition by Terry Orlick (Pantheon, 1978)

101 Best Family Card Games by Alfred Sheinwold (Sterling, 1992)

Having Fun Together: Creative Ideas for Families by Debbie Stapley (Bookcraft, 1992)

Sources for family games and activities include:

Family Pastimes
RR 4
Perth, Ontario, Canada K7H 3C6

Explorers Card Game
U.S. Games Systems, Inc
Stamford, CT 06902

Animal Town Game Company
P.O. Box 2002
Santa Barbara, CA 93120

Hearthsong
6519 N. Galena Road
P.O. Box 1773
Peoria, IL 61656-1773
1-800-325-2502

10. Ask Your Child's Opinion Once A Day

Time Cost:	5 minutes a day, per child
Resource Cost:	None

t is important for you to know what your child likes, dislikes, thinks, and values. But it is more important that your child know that his or her feelings and ideas are valued by you and by the rest of the family. This is the first step in understanding that the child's opinions will be valued by our democratic society, and this is a building block for self-esteem and independent thinking. Asking for and listening to your child's opinion also accomplishes a second, related function: In knowing that the opinion is valued, and in being asked to state it, the child practices critical thinking. He or she will learn over time and through practice, to present his or her opinions or feelings in a rational, justifiable, convincing manner. A third and very important function is served — a child learns that in an environment where his or her opinion is valued and important, that likewise the opinions of other people, however different or disagreeable they may be, are also important.

If, with the investment of five minutes a day, we could build self- esteem, democratic principles, critical thinking and tolerance, would we do it? I think we would, and of course we should. For starters, think about the following:

∞ Give your baby, toddler, young child and teenager choices. Every decision, from what to eat or not to eat, what to wear or not to wear, when and how to make the bed or clean the room — all of these tasks should be presented in terms of choices. Of course, you do not cater to the child's every whim. The choice may be to eat the dinner the family eats, or to go hungry. But let the child choose! The choice must be to wear clothing, but let the child choose what to wear (to the maximum extent possible). As a parent, we already have an incredible amount of control over our children; they are dependent upon us for just about everything. Within this framework, we must allow freedom to let the child develop his or her capabilities to decide.

∞ Ask the children what they'd like to do on weekends or certain evenings of the week. Consider their desires, try something different and you may just have a great time and learn something.

∞ Let your children help or totally plan some of the family's meals. This is a given in households where the children are preparing their own meals most nights anyway. In these cases, perhaps the parent should give the child a choice of meals that the parent prepares for them.

∞ Talk politics (local, national, and family) at the dinner table. Every member of the family has an opinion, so hear it out.

∞ Even when you know what you are going to do, such as the way you drive to school or work every day, think about occasionally asking for your child's input on the process. Play the "What if?" game.

∞ Encourage independence in your child by cultivating tolerance on your part. This means if your child selects a strange (to you) combination of clothing or hairstyle, refrain from criticism if you can. If he or she wants to make a peanut butter-celery-spaghetti sandwich, let it happen without sarcastic or cutting comments.

For further information on how to cultivate critical thinking and creating independence, check out the following:

I Wanna Do It Myself: From Baby to Toddler — A Radical Three-Tiered Approach to Helping Your Child Achieve Independence by William Sammons (Walt Disney Book Publications, 1992)

Raising Kids Who Can: Use Good Judgement, Assume Responsibility, Communicate Effectively, Respect Self and Others, Cooperate. Develop Self-Esteem and Enjoy Life by Betty Lou Bettner and Amy Lew (Connex Press, 1990)

Raising Kids Who Can: Using Family Meetings to Nurture Responsible, Cooperative, Caring and Happy Children by Betty Lou Bettner and Amy Lew (Harper Collins, 1992)

Empowering Your Child by C. F. Bateman (Hampton Roads Publishing Company, 1990)

One Hundred Educational Conversations Your Should Have With Your Child by Vito Perrone (Chesea House, 1993) (Twelve volumes, K/1 through Grade 12)

Raising Self-Reliant Children in a Self-Indulgent World: Seven Building Blocks for Developing Capable Young People by Stephen H. Glenn and Jane Nelson (Prima Publications, 1989)

Helping Kids Help Themselves by Perry E. Good (New View Publications, 1992)

Thinking Games to Play with Your Child: Easy Ways to Develop Creative and Critical Thinking Skills by Cheryl Tuttle, M. Ed. and Penny Paquette (Lowell House, 1991)

11. Make & Create With Your Child

Time Cost:	30 minutes a week, extra
Resource Cost:	$0 - $50

Your child should be exposed to craft materials and encouraged to create things for himself or herself. To complement that creativity inherent in our children, we should also involve our kids in things we ourselves make, create or do. Allowing your child to help you make things that you normally make is guaranteed to have several results:

> 1) It is guaranteed to take longer than it would if you did it alone;
>
> 2) It is guaranteed to make three times the mess than if you did it yourself; and
>
> 3) It is guaranteed to make your child happy (unless you are so annoyed by items 1 and 2 that you ruin it for everyone).

Making things with your child may take some thought, and perhaps some advanced planning, but for starters consider:

∞ Cooking breakfast, lunch or dinner, or baking treats with your child as key helper. Assistance can include anything from reading the recipe, measuring, dipping, and mixing, cleaning up, or doing it all with your supervision. Breaking eggs is particularly fun for children, and their little fingers are better than yours at getting tiny pieces of eggshell out of the cup. (Remember that!)

∞ Making costumes for school events, parties, and special holidays. Involve your child with ideas, gathering decorative accessories, sizing, and working with you in the construction of costumes. A costume that has part of the child himself in it goes a lot further than one you buy ready-made at the store.

∞ Make your own decorations for holidays and birthdays with your kids.

∞ If you need hooks or pictures put up in the house, let your child help by telling you where and how he or she thinks the hooks or pictures should be hung. Let the child help with selection and placement of pictures and other household decorations.

∞ Make your own curtains and have the children help pick out the material or patterns.

∞ Make your own air fresheners using oranges or lemons covered in cloves by having the children do it. Mix your own potpourri and have the children experiment with different combinations. Try creating your own scented candles, with the children's help.

For further information, look for the following books:

52 Simple Ways to Have Fun with Your Child by Stephen Arterburn and Carl Dreizler (Oliver-Nelson, 1991)

Indoor Sunshine: Great Things to Make and Do on Rainy Days by Diane Cherkerzian (Boyds Mills Press, 1993)

Outdoor Fun: Great Things to Make and Do on Sunny Days by Diane Cherkerzian (Boyds Mills Press, 1993)

12. Take Your Child To Work With You

Time Cost:	2-6 hours per year
Resource Cost:	None

At least once a year, you should bring your child to your place of work with you for a visit. Show your child what you do, how you earn your money, who your customer is, and tell him how you know when you've done a good job. Introduce your child to your boss, and your co-workers. Show your child where you keep your child's photographs and artwork. Show your child where you eat lunch, and where you buy snacks. No matter if you build roads, operate heavy equipment, type at a word processor, or supervise hundreds of factory workers, your child will gain valuable insight into you and what makes you tick. If you never show your child the work you do, then the 80% of waking hours your child has without you (i.e. while you are at work) remain vague and mysterious.

For more information, talk to your supervisor today!

13. Go To Lunch With Your Child

Time Cost:	2 to 4 hours per year
Resource Cost:	$2 to $30

You are welcome at your child's school, so plan on going to lunch with your child when you can. Check ahead of time, to be sure the school cafeteria will be open for you, then drop in, buy a lunch (or bring one) and eat with your child. Or, if you can't go to lunch with your kid, take him or her to lunch with you. The time lost from school during the lunch hour will be well worth it for everyone.

For more information, contact your child's teacher or school principal.

14. Make Sure Your Child Has Own Money

Time Cost:	5 minutes a week
Resource Cost:	$1 to $20 a week

There are many ways to ensure your child understands how to manage money, but the best way is to make sure he or she has some of their own. Whether this is done via allowances, collections of monetary gifts, or opportunities provided to earn money (or a combination of all three), it is important that the child have control over his or her personal money. There are only three things to remember when you consider your role as parent to a child with money:

1) It's their money;

2) It's their money, and;

3) It's their money.

These three rules translate to the following actions:

1) No matter what they buy, they have to be able to afford it.

2) No matter what they buy, it is theirs to keep.

3) No matter what they buy or how they spend, Mom or Dad doesn't bail them out with more money for the thing they "really" wanted.

If you do not adhere to the three actions, don't worry — you'll be raising future U.S. Congressmen and women. (That's a joke, I think). But seriously, the biggest mistake parents make when their kids have money, regardless of the source, is trying to have their cake and eat it too. We want to make sure they have money, but we want it to be our money at the same time. We can't have it both ways. For more information of teaching kids to manage and work with money, check out the following books:

Raising Money-Smart Kids by Ron and Judy Blue (Nelson, 1992)

The Money Book for Kids by Nancy Burgeson (Troll Associates, 1991)

Kids and Cash: Solving a Parent's Dilemma by Ken Davis and Tom Taylor (Bantam, 1981)

Children's Money-Making Jobs by Jodi Jill (J.J. Features, 1993)

Kids Can Make Money, Too! How Young People Can Succeed Financially —Over 200 Ways to Earn Money and How to Make it Grow by Vada L. Jones (Calico Press, 1988)

Kid Cash: Creative Money-Making Ideas (Grades 4-7) by Joe Lamancusa (TAB Books, 1993)

Money Doesn't Grow on Trees: A Parent's Guide to Raising Financially Responsible Children by Neale S. Godfrey (Chairman of the Children's Financial Network) and Carolina Edwards (A Fireside Book/Simon & Schuster, 1994)

Better Than a Lemonade Stand! Small Business Ideas for Kids
by Daryl Bernstein (a seventeen-year-old entrepreneur, author, speaker, and advocate for young people. Having run many small businesses since the age of eight, he authored his first book at the age of fifteen.) (Beyond Words Publishing, 1992) To order: 1-800-284-9673

Or write to these organizations:

Credit Union National Association
Box 431
Madison, WI 53701

National Association Of Investment Clubs
1515 E. Eleven Mile Road
Royal Oak, MI 48067

Money Management Institute
2700 Sanders Road
Prospect Heights, IL 60070

Junior Achievement, Inc
45 E. Clubhouse Drive
Colorado Springs, CO 80906
(719) 540-8000

Or call 1-800-403-KIDS for a free handbook, "Liberty Financial Young Investors Parent's Guide," published by Liberty Financial Group.

15. Plant Something Yearly With Your Child

Time Cost:	2 to 10 hours a year
Resource Cost:	0 to $30 annually

Whether you have a window box, a front or back yard garden, or a farm, get your child involved in growing plants every year. Gardening is fun, easy to do, and it can be inexpensive. It is a great way to expose your children to science, experimentation, responsibility, and the environment. Some ideas to consider include:

- Grow vegetables from seeds in pots, buckets, barrels, or window boxes.

- Grow flowers in your yard or on the windowsill. Try annuals, perennials, or bulb types. Choose flowers that will not cause allergies. Allow your children to help you or let them be in charge.

- Experiment with exotic or tropical plants in your home.

• Build a terrarium, using a gallon jar or an old glass aquarium.

• Start a compost heap. Using woven fencing material, blocks, or a medium-sized barrel, create a small area to locate your compost. Have your kids collect table waste, clippings, cut grass, and other organic matter to add to the heap. Using a shovel or pitchfork, turn the material once a week or so. Keep it damp, but not soggy. Once composted, use the material to enrich your flowerboxes and garden areas.

• Start seeds from the fruits and vegetables that your family eats. Keep this operation small and observable in a kitchen or a child's bedroom. Place the seeds and a few drops of water in sealed plastic bags; then watch for germination. Cardboard egg cartons make good seed containers—they are biodegradable and the seedlings can be easily transplanted into larger containers or outdoors without a mess. Remember to water the plants well at the time of transplanting. Here are some ideas to get you started:

∞ Apple, pear, and cherry: Freeze seeds for several weeks, then soak in water for a day, then plant. To see the progress, let seeds germinate in a moist, sealed plastic bag or folded clear plastic wrap.

∞ Avocado: Insert three toothpicks halfway into the middle of the avocado seed, such that the seed can rest on the toothpicks in a small cup or glass. Place the avocado seed into a cup or glass, with the narrow or pointed end down. Fill cup or glass with water up to the level just below the toothpicks, and place in a windowsill.

∞ Citrus fruits (orange, lemon, lime): Soak seeds for a day, then plant in moistened sandy soil. Cover container with plastic wrap to prevent drying out.

∞ Melons, squash, and pumpkin: Clean and dry seeds, then plant in light, damp soil. If desired, transplant to larger container or garden when plants are a few inches high.

∞ Carrots: Cut off carrot top, and place in container of light or sandy soil. Keep damp until root growth starts.

∞ Garlic: Take a clove from a bulb of garlic. Place in light damp soil and watch it grow.

∞ Potato: Let a potato grow eyes (most old potatoes, when kept in the dark, will produce growths called eyes). Cut the potato in pieces, with at least one eye per potato piece. Plant these in egg carton size or larger containers. These are easily grown outside as well during spring, summer, and fall.

∞ Tomato: Clean and dry seeds, and plant in light, dampened soil. Transplant into larger containers when a few inches high.

∞ Dry beans: Soak for a day, then either plant in damp soil, or allow to germinate in clear plastic bags with a few drops of water. Try all kinds. If you want to transplant outside, most beans are vine-type plants that need a structure (fence or wall) for support.

∞ Popcorn: Allow to germinate in a clear, moistened plastic bag, or plant in damp soil. If you transplant, place in sunny area, at least a foot apart.

∞ Sunflower seeds: Using raw, uncooked, unshelled seeds, plant in light, moist soil in a sunny area. If planted in egg carton sections and transplanted later, plant at least a foot apart in a sunny area.

• Try rooting cuttings from shrubs or other plants you admire. Cut a fresh twig-sized piece, at an angle, and keep in a moist sand/peat mixture. Use a commercial root stimulating agent if desired, and be patient. Good candidates for cuttings include roses and azealeas.

• Plant a tree every year. Get live Christmas trees and plant them afterward. If you have no place to plant a tree, talk to someone at your local community center, church, or park and ask for permission and advice on tree planting.

For more information see the following:

Books:

500 Terrific Ideas for Gardening by Anne Hulpin (Round Stone Press, Inc, 1992)

Sunflower Houses: Garden Discoveries for Children of All Ages by Sharon Lovejoy (Interweave Press, 1991)

Gardening Projects for Children by Tanya Bigge (Murdoch Books, 1992)

Gardening from Garbage: How to Grow Plants from Recycled Kitchen Scraps by Judith F. Handelsman (Millbrook Press, 1993)

Grow It! An Indoor-Outdoor Gardening Guide for Kids by Erika Markmann (Random Books for Young Readers, 1991)

Let's Get Growing: Twenty-five Quick and Easy Gardening Projects for Kids by Joel Rapp (Crown, 1992)

In a Pumpkin Shell: Over Twenty Pumpkin Projects for Kids (Grade K-4) by Jennifer S. Gillis (Garden City Publications, 1992)

Fun With Fruits and Vegetable by Patricia Lief (Fearon Teaching Aids, 1991)

Trees Every Boy and Girl Should Know, Fourth Edition, American Forestry Association Staff (American Forestry Association, 1977)

Organizations:

National Arbor Day Foundation
100 Arbor Avenue
Nebraska City, NE 68410
(402) 474-5655

National Gardening Association
180 Flynn Avenue
Burlington, VT 05401-5401
(802) 863-1308

American Community Garden Association
C/O the Chicago Botanic Garden
Glencoe, IL 60022
(312) 835-0250

Garden Clubs of America
598 Madison Avenue
New York, NY 10022-1614
(212) 753-8287

Sources:

Global Releaf
8555 Plummer Road
Jacksonville, FL 32219
1-800-677-0727

(Sells trees that are direct offsprings of original trees located on historic sites. Certificate of authenticity and history is provided with each tree.)

W. Atlee and Burpee Company
Warminster, PA 18974
1-800-888-1447

(Offers "FunSeed for Kids Garden Kits.")

Mellinger's Inc.
2310 W. South Range Road
North Lima, OH 44452-9731

(Publishes a seed catalog, including a special kid's page with books, seed packs, and a "backyard explorer kit.")

Park Seed Company
Cokesbury Road
Greenwood, S.C. 29647-0001

(Free catalog, provides a "Children's Choice Seed Collection and Garden Contest" annually.)

The Cook's Garden
P.O. Box 535
Londonderry, VT 05148
(802) 824-3400

(Offers special collections of seeds for kids.)

Ripley's Believe It Or Not
World's Most Unusual Seed Catalog
10 Bay Street
Westport, CT 06880

($1 catalog with unusual seeds and gigantic vegetables.)

Garden Kids Family
Alberta Nurseries Seeds, Ltd
P.O. Box 20 (FC3)
Bowden, Alberta, Canada
T0M-0K0

Gardens for Growing People
P.O. Box 630
Point Reyes, CA 94956
(415) 663-9433

SECTION THREE

SUPPORTING OUR SCHOOLS

You want your child to do well in school, in relationships, and in life. What can you do to see that your child's time in school is quality time? How can you (with your busy schedule and with only limited access to the school system) positively influence your child's school environment? The good news is that you *can* do a lot!

Read further for a variety of effective and inexpensive ways to make a difference in your child's school experience.

1. Provide Your Child With A Study Area

Time Cost:	1 hour a year
Resource Cost:	$0 to $150, one time cost

Your kids are in school for at least thirteen years, and many of them more. Homework is increasingly being required by our public schools in an attempt to improve the levels of student achievement. But homework is only a small reason for your child to have a place to study in his own home. The big reason is to communicate to your child that it is important to do brainwork, even though (and precisely because) brainwork is difficult. You as parent need to show your kid that you understand that brainwork is tough, and you're doing your part as provider and creator of the home.

For the price of four or five compact disks or a family dinner out, a small desk can be acquired; less if you buy a used one. If you don't buy CDs or eat out, and don't think you can get a desk, you can set aside access to the kitchen table before and after dinner for the child's use in pursuing academic studies. Remember that brainwork takes energy, and wherever your child's study area is, that it's <u>not</u> a "no-food and drink" zone. Your attitude is an important factor in your child's development of good study habits.

Some tips to help your child study at home include:

∞ Communicate to your child that home study and homework is important to you. Show an interest in what your child has been assigned. Don't try to do the homework, rather support your child's efforts by locating reference materials, bringing a snack, and perhaps keeping younger siblings away from the study area while homework is being done.

∞ Make sure your child has materials to complete homework readily available. Paper, pencils, pens, markers, scissors, tape, stapler, ruler, paper clips, and glue should be kept together for ready access near the study area. Keep these items in a small box, plastic storage bin, or decorative basket, with the child's name on it if possible.

∞ If homework is assigned regularly, this is a regular opportunity to send the teacher notes and written comments. Express your questions or concerns or send kudos or ideas to your child's teachers using the homework assignment process as a medium. Make this type of communication between you and your child's teachers a habit. It helps everyone, and shows your child by your actions, that homework and home study is important.

∞ Have a place in the house that completed homework is kept the night before. Make a habit of looking at your kids homework, even if you do this late at night or early in the morning. This helps you stay in touch with what's happening, or possibly, with what may not be happening.

Resources to help you help your children include:

Books:

Ending the Homework Hassle: How to Help Your Child Succeed Independently in School by John Rosemond (Andrews & McMeel, 1990)

Taming the Homework Monster: How to Make Homework a Positive Learning Experience for Your Child by Ellen Klavan (Poseidon Press, 1992)

52 Ways to Help Your Child Do Better in School by Jon Dargaty (Oliver-Nelson, 1993)

Parent's Guide to Helping Kids Become "A" Students by Anne Farrell (Bluse Bird Publishers, 1990)

Up the Learning Ladder: How to Boost Your Child's Study Power by Lois D. Glass (Carriage Press, 1988)

Homework Helpers: A Guide for Parents Offering Assistance by Joan E. Kuepper (Education Media Group, 1987)

Mail order sources of children's furniture:

Conron's Mail Order
475 Oberlin Avenue South
Lakewood, NJ 08701-1053
(201) 905-8800

Country Workshop
95 Rome Street
Newark, NJ 07105
(201) 589-3407 or 1-800-526-8001

Crate and Barrel
P.O. Box 3057
Northbrook, IL 60065-3057
(312) 272-3112

Environments, Inc
P.O. Box 1348
Beaufort Industrial Park
Beaufort, S.C. 29901-1348
1-800-EI-CHILD (342-4453)

Educational Teaching Aids
199 Carpenter Avenue
Wheeling, IL 60090
(312) 520-2500

H.U.D.D.L.E.
11159 Santa Monica Blvd
Los Angeles, CA 90025
(213) 836-8001

J.L. Hammett Company
30 Hammett Place
Braintree , MA 02184
(617) 848-1000

2. Know Goals Of Your Child's School

Time Cost:	30 minutes every September
Resource Cost:	None

Can you name five or ten outputs, or even one or two outputs of your child's education process? School goals should be published at least annually in the local newspaper, as well as listed in the parent-student handbooks and other school documentation. If you can't find a set of school goals and standards for your child's school, then ask for them.

School goals should establish clear and non-numerical success criteria. This can be part of the school's mission, aims, or purposes. The American Association of School Administrators, in their pamphlet "Creating Quality Schools," lists some examples of school aims and purposes, as follows:

∞ To create lifetime learners
∞ To develop students who enjoy learning

∞ To graduate productive members of society

∞ To produce employable people

∞ To foster people committed to cooperation with other people

∞ To develop continually improving learners

∞ To provide increasing benefits for everyone in the community

Notice that the sample aims and purposes of school have an indirect, non-numerical value or measurement. These criteria can be used by each teacher and each administrator in a school system as a measure of value in what they are doing on a daily basis. Did my high school graduate 75.4% of the pool of potential graduates based on the freshmen class rolls four years prior, or did my school make progress toward graduating productive people? In reality, communities care more about the tangible meaning and value of a high school diploma than about the fact that a graduate has one.

Parents need to participate in the establishment of school aims and purposes, as well as to define success criteria more clearly. Real success criteria (defined as what we really want from the school system) will have only one numerical value — 100%. Do we, the parents, really want a 90% graduation rate for our high school or do we want our child to graduate? Do we really want our school to compete on national tests where our school's average school-wide performance is above 50% of all other school's school-wide average performance, or do we want our child to excel? The honest answer must be that we want our own children to excel, to learn, to achieve and be productive, employable citizens.

We also need to redefine failure non-numerically. The famous Thomas Edison response, when queried as to how it felt to have tried over a thousand ways to make a light bulb, with every method having failed, put the concept of failure into its true perspective. Edison defined failure as a means to discovery. He had learned a thousand ways a light bulb could not be made. The ability and privilege to experience failure and use it to succeed is a most valuable lesson. The emphasis on grade level achievement and norming, the practice of academic tracking based on expectations of students formed years earlier by the system, the emphasis on grading by both teachers, students, and parents, all are inhibiters to true success.

If you have questions about the school's goals and objectives, go to your child's school and talk to the administrator. Ask for the parent handbook and other documentation. For more information about school goals and objectives, see the following:

Books:

Good Schools: What Makes Them Work by Cynthia Tursman (National School Press, 1981)

Inside American Education: The Decline, the Deception, the Dogma by Thomas Sowell (Free Press, 1992)

School Savvy by Dianne Harrington and Laurette Young (FS&G, 1993)

The School-Smart Parent by Gene I. Maeroff (H. Holt & Co., 1990)

Who Pushed Humpty-Dumpty? by Donald Barr (Atheneum, 1972)

Organizations:

American Association of School Administrators
1801 N. Moore Street
Arlington, VA 22209
(703) 528-0700

Association for Childhood Education International
11141 Georgia Avenue, Suite 200
Wheaton, MD 20902
(301) 942-2443

National Assoc. for the Education of Young Children
1509 16th Street, NW
Washington, DC 20036
1-800-424-2460

National Association of Elementary School Principals
1615 Duke Street
Alexandria, VA 22314
(703) 684-3345

National Association of Secondary School Principals
1904 Association Drive
Reston, VA 22091
(703) 860-0200

National Association of State Boards of Education
701 North Fairfax Street, Suite 340
Alexandria, VA 22314
(703) 684-4000

3. Evaluate Your Child's School

Time Cost:	20 minutes each school quarter
Resource Cost:	$0 to $1 (if you make copies of this feedback sheet and mail it to your school)

P arents need to have a way of measuring their child's school and schooling and evaluating it in terms that will result in improved school performance. Most schools offer opportunities for feedback via parent-teacher conferences, parent nights, and open houses. Unfortunately, many of us do not really know how to articulate our concerns and feedback in a regular way to teachers and school administration.

One way to help generate useful feedback is via a checklist or questionnaire. Following is a sample evaluation sheet, that can be used as a starting point in your evaluation of your childrens' schools. This one, or another like it, can be provided directly to your child's teacher or principal, or just used as a guide in preparation for an upcoming parent teacher conference. Reviewing the questions and answering them, with your child's assistance, will help you begin to think about public education in a critical and productive way. Instead of a passive consumer, you become an informed and active customer.

Sample School Feedback / Evaluation Sheet

Please circle the number that best describes your feelings about the
following areas:

	Strongly Disagree	Strongly Agree	No Opinion

1. I understand the goals and objectives of
this school   1 2 3 4 5   0

2. I am happy with the class curriculum and
academic standards in my child's classes,
as follows:

a. Mathematics/Geometry   1 2 3 4 5   0
b. English and Language Arts   1 2 3 4 5   0
c. Biology and Physical Science   1 2 3 4 5   0
d. Health and Physical Fitness   1 2 3 4 5   0
e. Foreign Language   1 2 3 4 5   0
f. Other _____   1 2 3 4 5   0
g. Other _____   1 2 3 4 5   0
h. Other _____   1 2 3 4 5   0

3. I am happy with the classroom size and
teacher's instructional program in my child's
classes, as follows:

a. Mathematics/Geometry   1 2 3 4 5   0
b. English and Language Arts   1 2 3 4 5   0
c. Biology and Physical Science   1 2 3 4 5   0
d. Health and Physical Fitness   1 2 3 4 5   0
e. Foreign Language   1 2 3 4 5   0
f. Other _____   1 2 3 4 5   0
g. Other _____   1 2 3 4 5   0
h. Other _____   1 2 3 4 5   0

Sample School Feedback / Evaluation Sheet (continued)

	Strongly Disagree		Strongly Agree		No Opinion

4. I am happy with the classroom discipline in my child's classes, as follows:

a. Mathematics/Geometry	1	2	3	4	5	0
b. English and Language Arts	1	2	3	4	5	0
c. Biology and Physical Science	1	2	3	4	5	0
d. Health and Physical Fitness	1	2	3	4	5	0
e. Foreign Language	1	2	3	4	5	0
f. Other _____	1	2	3	4	5	0
g. Other _____	1	2	3	4	5	0
h. Other _____	1	2	3	4	5	0

5. I am satisfied with the availability of materials in the school library.   1   2   3   4   5   0

6. I am satisfied with the appearance and general condition of the school facilities and grounds.   1   2   3   4   5   0

7. I feel that my child's teacher is accessible and receptive to my concerns and ideas.   1   2   3   4   5   0

8. The parent-teacher organization is effective.   1   2   3   4   5   0

9. I think the principal and school board are receptive to my ideas and concerns.   1   2   3   4   5   0

10. The thing I like best about this school is ....

11. The thing I like least about this school is ....

12. If I could change one thing about the school right now, it would be....

Name (optional but recommended):_____

Date:_____

Student's Name (optional): _____

Daytime phone: _____   Evening phone: _____

For additional information, see the following:

Books:

Raising Standards in Schools: Problems and Solutions by Patricia Pine (American Association of School Administrators /AASA, 1985)

A Parent's Survival Guide to the Public Schools by Sally D. Reed (National Council for Better Education, 1991)

Schooling Options: Choosing the Best for You and Your Child by Elain K. McEwan (Shaw Publications, 1991)

"Choosing a School for Your Child" Free pamphlet developed by the U.S. Dept of Education Office of Research and Improvement. Write to Consumer Information Center, Pueblo, CO 81002

Organizations:

National Congress of Parents and Teachers (National PTA)
700 North Rush Street
Chicago, IL 60611-2571
(312) 787-0977

Publishes *PTA Magazine* (7 issues per year) and *Looking In On Your School: A Workbook For Improving Public Education* (1982)

National Council for Better Education
1800 Diagonal Road
Alexandria, VA 22314

Alliance for Parental Involvement in Education, Inc.
P.O. Box 59
East Chatham, N.Y. 12060-0059
(518) 392-6900

National Center for Restructuring Education, Schools, and Teaching
Teacher's College,
Columbia University
25 W. 120th Street
New York, NY 10027

4. Demand a Lot of Your School's Newsletter

Time Cost:	15 to 30 minutes a week
Resource Cost:	None

Schools normally publish monthly, bimonthly, even weekly newsletters. Sometimes, parent-teacher organizations or other groups affiliated with the school publish newsletters. Individual teachers often send home newsletters periodically with their students. First, you should be reading these newsletters when you get them. Make sure you're getting them in a timely manner, and then look critically at the contents. Types of information you need to be looking for (and finding) in your school newsletter include:

- Academic achievements of students
- Testing schedules
- State or federal changes that affect the school or schooling
- School expenditures and also need for supplies and materials
- The school's ongoing "wish list" of parental assistance or expertise, curriculum items, or real property

- A question of the week or month column
- Schedule of school board as well as parent-teacher meetings
- Parenting hints and tips
- Explanations of school policies and new teaching techniques
- Points of contact listing
- Reprints of media articles of education interest can be used in newsletters and newsletter attachments
- Current listing of desired gift subscriptions and book purchases for the library or teacher's lounge
- The school principal's phone and fax number
- Phone numbers for special offices that have information or need assistance
- Course descriptions for standard and special courses offered

If you are not satisfied with the newsletters you're receiving (or you aren't receiving any), ask questions. Find out which organizations or entities are publishing a newsletter, and volunteer to help them. Provide your feedback and input as to the types of things you'd like to see published. With the many home computers and easy-to-use word processing and desk-top publishing software available today, putting out a newsletter can be as simple as volunteering your time to the parent-teacher organization or in the school administrative office. If you can't help out that way, ask the question anyway. For more information on school communications, look for the following:

Improving Home-School Communications by Edward E. Gotts and Richard F. Purnell (Phi Delta Kappan, 1985)

Creating Newsletters, Brochures, and Pamphlets by Barbara R. Rodke and Barbara L. Stein (Neal-Schuman, 1992)

5. Establish a School Improvement Council

Time Cost:	3 to 10 hours a quarter
Resource Cost:	$0 to $20 annually

P articipate in a school improvement council or group, or work to establish one. A school improvement council or group can bring interested parents, teachers, and administrators together to establish goals, act as a clearinghouse for ideas, and provide a focus to long-term school improvement. The council should include representatives for parents, teachers, administrators, students, local government, and local businesses.

The school improvement council should be a subset or expansion of existing infrastructure, perhaps including school board members, administrators, and members of the parent-teacher organizations and local Chamber of Commerce. If a group or council exists to focus on school improvement, then join it and be a part of it. If not, forming a new group sounds like a tough thing to do; it requires leadership, energy, and vision.

A few points about these qualities:

∞ Leadership is what you already show every day as head or co-head of your household. You, as a responsible parent, are already a leader. In your family, you make things happen, you discover new ways and teach them. You shape and mold your family members' attitudes, and you have a strong relationship to each of them. *You are already a leader.*

∞ Energy is a strange thing — the less you do the less energy you have. The more you do, the more energy you have. The key is in the definition of the word "do." I prefer the Webster's Encyclopedic Unabridged Dictionary definition number 13: "to create, form, or bring into being." The more of these things that you "do" in your limited time, the greater your energy level.

∞ Vision, in the sense of being able to visualize an improvement or an improved condition, is something you may not think you have. Think though: Do you have any opinions on the speed limit around a school zone, or the placement of stop lights? How about the way the local television news presents its reports? How about zoning rules near your home, or air pollution, or gun control? If you have an opinion, and you can verbalize it, then you have a vision of how things "oughtta be."

Now that we have gotten that out of the way, the following organizations and references may be able to help:

Books:

Fulfilling the Promise of Excellence: A Practitioner's Guide to School Improvement by Richard Dufour and Robert Eaker (Wilkerson Publishing Company, 1987)

We Must Take Charge: The Schools and Our Future by Chester E. Finn (MacMillan, 1991)

Schools That Work by Judith Gelber (Uriel Publications, 1990)

School Improvement in an Era of Change by David Hopkins and Mel Ainscon (Cassell, 1993)

Partnership for Improving Schools by Byrd L. Jones and Robert W. Maloy (Greenwood, 1988)

Developing Leadership for Parent-Citizen Groups by Crystal Kuykendall (National Committee for Citizens in Education, 1976)

Organizations:

Project Public Life
Humphrey Institute
University of Minnesota
310 19th Avenue South
Minneapolis, MN 55455
(612) 625-6142

Council for the Advancement
and Support of Education
11 Dupont Circle, NW Suite 400
Washington, DC 20036-1261

Family Resource Coalition
200 South Michigan Avenue
Suite 1520
Chicago, IL 60604-2404
(312) 341-0900

Provides information on starting or finding parent's groups

Alliance for Parental
Involvement in
Education, Inc.
P.O. Box 59
East Chatham, N.Y. 12060-0059
(518) 392-6900

National Coalition for Parent
Involvement in Education
Box 39
1201-16th Street, NW
Washington, D.C. 20036

The Parent Power Foundation
1010 W. Orange Grove Road
Tucson, AZ 85704

American Association of
Parents and Children
560 Herndon Parkway, Suite 110
Herndon, VA 22070

6. Participate in Your School's Suggestion Program

Time Cost:	15 minutes monthly
Resource Cost:	$0 to $20 annually

Every school, and every government agency, should have an active suggestion program. Your school should have one, and the following questions should be answered (preferably by a "yes"):

1) Are procedures for suggesting policy changes clear and easy?
2) Are "suggestion" forms for policy changes or amendments provided to parents, students, and teachers?
3) Are suggestion boxes publicized, and conveniently located for students, teachers, and parents?
4) Are suggestions processed quickly? By whom? Is school accountability maintained?

To improve and increase participation in the school's suggestion program, consider:

∞ Providing preaddressed suggestion forms to principals and teachers. These can be printed and made available to parents, including by sending them home with students routinely.

∞ Establishing accessible school mailboxes for School Board members and principals. School board members and school and district administrators should have mail boxes in every school front office. The mailboxes should be out in a central area where parents, teachers, and students can access them, and should be postage free when dropped off at any school in the school district.

∞ Providing preaddressed envelopes to parents at registration. Provide preaddressed envelopes, postcards, or fold and mail feedback or comment sheets to parents at registration or at the beginning of the school year. Several of these handed out, and routinely sent home with students would allow administrators and principals to hear from people who otherwise are too busy to hunt down the address or phone number. It also communicates to parents that their concerns are important and valid.

Tip: The local parent-teacher organization could make this an annual project at minimal cost, and could also distribute their own self-addressed feedback sheets to improve parental involvement.

For more information on providing customer feedback effectively to school management, write to these organizations:

Citizen's Education Center, NW
310 1st Avenue South
Number 330
Seattle, WA 98104-2536

Institute for Responsive Education
605 Commonwealth Ave
Boston, MA 02215
(617) 353-3309

The Parent Power Foundation
1010 W. Orange Grove Road
Tucson, AZ 85704

National Coalition for Parent Involvement in Education
Box 39
1201 16th Street NW
Washington, D.C. 20036

7. Create A "Parent Center" In School

Time Cost:	5 to 10 hours a month
Resource Cost:	Zero to $100

T he Ellis School in Boston created a parent center — a room for parents in the school — that was a low-cost success. This parent center was staffed by two paid coordinators (both parents) and a number of unpaid volunteers. Parents dropped in for coffee, a chat and information. The center sponsored Graduate Equivalent Degree (GED) and English as a Second Language (ESL) classes for parents. Other activities of the parent center included:

∞ Hosted grade level breakfasts that brought together teachers, administrators and family members to talk informally in a non-threatening atmosphere about curriculum, grade level objectives, and classroom concerns.

∞ Sponsored breakfasts for fathers, designed to bring the male family members to school and into the educational process.

∞ Served as an escort and referral service for parents with special needs.

∞ Organized a clothing exchange and a "school-on-a-cart" that contained teaching materials for parental use.

∞ Organized a small library of books and toys for children.

∞ Recruited parent volunteers.

The basic requirements for a parent center like the one implemented by Ellis School include a dedicated physical space, adult-sized tables and chairs, a paid staff of parents, a telephone, and a coffee pot. The entire operation was low cost and very beneficial for the school and the educational process. A computer, modem and extra line could be installed in the facility to allow the use and accessing of any educational resources accessable through a computer network. Just about everything required to set up a parent center in your school could be donated by the community, school, local business, and by parents themselves.

For more information see the following books:

Activities for Parent's Groups by Gary Wilson (Humanics LTD, 1993)

Raising Funds for Your Child's School: Over Sixty Great Ideas for Parents and Teachers by Cynthia F. Gensheimer (Walker and Company, 1993)

Parent Programs and Open Houses by Susan Spaete (Building Blocks, 1987)

Or write to these organizations:

**National Association of
Partners in Education**
209 Madison Street, Suite 401
Alexandria, VA 22314
(703) 836-4880

Alliance for Parental Involvement in Education
P.O. Box 59
East Chatham, NY 12060-0059

National Coalition for Parent Involvement in Education
Box 39
1201 16th Street, NW
Washington, D.C. 20036

8. Use School Libraries

Time Cost:	30 minutes a week
Resource Cost:	Zero

Parents should frequently visit and use school libraries. Libraries in schools today are known as media centers, and often contain computers, videos, and a variety of learning tools and resources. Parents should be encouraged to borrow from school libraries, and to volunteer to work in them. This approach will bring parents physically to school, creates in parents a sense of ownership, and allows parents firsthand to evaluate where resources may be lacking, and see firsthand how they might help. Some ideas to consider include:

∞ Work as a parent to extend library hours (later at night, on weekends and throughout the summer). Encourage other parents to come in and browse. Parent, high school, college, and community volunteers may supervise, open and close the library on weekends and summer hours for no additional cost.

∞ Establish a program for home-loan of school computers, learning software, books, records, VCRs and educational tapes.

∞ Create in the school library a section devoted specifically to parents, containing books, tapes, videotapes and materials on home school activities, creative family crafts and projects, parenting, balancing family and work, etc. (See Section 4 for more details regarding parent education.)

∞ Ensure the library has a prominently displayed bulletin board that contains school happenings, customer feedback sheets, suggestion box, and the school's current "Wish List."

∞ Supplement the school libraries by using a book and materials donations "drop box" for community donations of books, records, computers and computer software, even videos.

∞ Hold parent assistance and informational meetings in school libraries after school.

For more information on how to help your school libraries, and to better use them, see the following books:

The Library -Classroom Connection by Silvana Carletti (Heinemann Ed, 1991)

If You Want to Evaluate Your Library, 2nd Ed by F.W. Lancaster (University of Illinois, 1993)

Setting Up a Library: How to Begin or Begin Again by Ruth S. Smith (CSLA, 1987)

When Your Library Budget is Almost Zero by Lesley S. Farmer (Linworth Publications, 1993)

Or write to:
American Library Association Public Information Office
50 E. Huron Street, Chicago, IL 60611

9. Make Sure Local Media Supports Education

Time Cost:	15 minutes a week
Resource Cost:	Zero

Your local paper probably has plenty about local high school sports, and it probably publishes the honor roll, along with letters to Santa, and pictures of the local Easter Egg Hunt. Is this the only kind of coverage of school issues that you need? Local papers should cover education issues thoroughly, routinely, and intelligently. If you don't think your local paper does this, then call, write, or send an electronic mail message to the editor or TV station manager, and suggest the following:

• Meeting dates, times, and locations of school board, parent-teacher organization, and other educational meetings be published in advance.

• The names of parents active in the parent-teacher organization, as well as the school principals and board members, be published, including their special areas of responsibility, phone and fax numbers.

• A weekly school question and answer segment be provided, with questions coming from the community and answers provided by the school superintendent or principal.

• Individual photos of academic award winners be photographed or posed in the spirit of the achievement, as are sports photographs. For example, publish shots of science winners showing their science projects or inventions, or their published book of poetry, or students debating at a podium.

• Just as pictures of school sports teams are published with their coaches, a group of students who have accomplished something that challenged their minds academically or scientifically should be pictured <u>with their teachers or mentors.</u>

• Incorporate school children and their interests into local media. Have children on the local news, not just news spots, but presenting news and weather, and doing interviews.

• Many middle and secondary schools already put together video yearbooks and weekly school news spots. This kind of work should also be shared with the community via local channels and cable TV.

• Publish examples of school students creative writing and poetry, on a routine basis. Not just once a year when papers publish letters to Santa, but a small section once a month or weekly to provide opportunity for recognition and showcasing of creative or editorial writing talent in the public schools.

Some examples of how local media has assisted schools and education are listed below:

∞ WWOR-TV, Secaucus, New Jersey, was recognized for its "A+ For Kids" project, a station-wide initiative designed to look at the problems and promise of our children's education. The project aims to inspire increased business, community and parental involvement while providing support for teachers. On-air activities include news segments, public service announcements, and primetime specials on education. Off-air, the station has created an "A+ For Kids" teacher network, whereby outstanding teaching ideas are shared. The station adopted one of New Jersey's most troubled high schools. (Thousand Points of Light #12, 8 Dec 1989)

∞ KIRO, Inc of Seattle, WA (a division of Bonneville International Corporation, a commercial broadcasting and media communications corporation) devotes over 18,000 hours of community service each year. KIRO participates in two educational programs: "Partnership in Public Education" (KIRO employees teach students about media and broadcasting); and "Junior Statesmen" (interested students learn the role of the media in politics). (Thousand Points of Light # 507, 12 July 1991)

∞ The Lawrence Eagle Tribune, of Lawrence, Massachusetts, realizes that media institutions have the ability to shape public attitudes, heighten awareness, and mobilize people for action. The newspaper began its own community service recognition program in February 1988, honoring local volunteers every day in its pages. Nominations for the newspaper's series come from local individuals, churches, synagogues, schools, colleges and hospitals. (Thousand Points of Light # 18, 15 Dec 1989)

Contact your principal, school board, local teacher's unions, newspaper editors, and cable stations with your concerns about education and the media. Some education-related national syndication publications include the following:

"Ask the Teachers" contains parental advice on education. Available from Davy Associates Media Features, 215 Del Mar, Suite G, San Clemente, CA 92672.

"The Mini Page" by Betty Debnam, contains activities and educational info for children. Available from Universal Press Syndicate, United Press International, 4900 Main Street, Kansas City, MO 64112.

"Education Today" from Southern Families, 3600 Fort, Waco, TX 76710.

10. Share Your Expertise at Your Child's School

Time Cost:	30 to 60 minutes a week
Resource Cost:	None

Every parent has something to offer, and every classroom can make time for parent volunteers. Share your skills in your child's classroom. This sharing can take many forms, from the traditional cupcakes to more effective in-class or after-class tutoring and leading or demonstrating special skills or projects.

To facilitate in-class sharing, ensure your child's teacher knows what you're interested in and any special skills you are willing to share at the beginning of the school year. One way to do this is to push your school to establish, if they haven't already, a complete parent resource listing. When the students register at the beginning of the school year, parents should likewise register their skills, hobbies, and special qualifications or interest areas.

There are many examples of how parents and other volunteers assist effectively in schools. Consider the examples below for ideas and inspiration:

∞ Torrey Pines Elementary School, near San Diego, California, implemented a **hands-on science program** developed and conducted by parent volunteers. Four to six parents came to school once a week to spend one and a half hours leading small groups of students in science activities. The groups covered a single topic, such as space, ecology, or earth science, every six weeks. Such programs are low budget, can be implemented by teachers and parents on a small scale (even by classroom), and they are effective for improving curriculum and getting parents involved in schools.

∞ Every Wednesday for the past fifteen years, Mr Almon Madigan, of West Granby, Connecticut, has hosted a **"reading hour"** for the Valley Preschool students. After greeting him enthusiastically, the children line up with books in hand, waiting a turn to hear "Grandpa Madigan" read to them. For many of these children, he serves as a surrogate grandfather. (Thousand Points of Light #769, 11 May 1992)

∞ Mr Erick Sutherland, of Bradenton, Florida, started by offering free tennis lessons to some youngsters at a tennis court. Mr Sutherland, a retired tennis professional, realized that **teaching tennis** was a tool to capture the attention of children. In 1988, he founded the International Youth Tennis Foundation to provide positive activities for young people. Each summer, he coordinates a free tennis camp, through which he provides tennis lessons and classes in reading, writing, and spelling. During the school year, Mr Sutherland gives tennis lessons after school and on weekends. (Thousand Points of Light # 368, 1 Feb 1991)

∞ In 1991, Ms Irene Dixon-Darnell, of Reno, Nevada, launched a unique pilot program to enhance the learning skills of students at Virginia Palmer Elementary School. She visits the school for five hours every day to teach chess to fourteen classes. Through the **game of chess**, Ms Dixon-Darnell believes that students learn to discipline their minds and increase their ability to concentrate, think logically, and solve problems. She has reached over 300 students, many of whom come from low-income families. School officials have noted that study habits and clasroom conduct have improved among the youngsters involved in this program. (Thousand Points of Light # 793, 7 Jun 1992)

∞ Police Captain Al Lewis, of Philadelphia, Pennsylvania, has gone above and beyond his official duties to promote literacy. He initiated a **tutorial program** for young people in his neighborhood, whereby police officers tutor students in basic reading and writing. The officers meet with the students once a week at the Police Department, fostering understanding between officers and young citizens of the community. Capt Lewis has also established a public library in response to the need to increase literacy and promote neighborhood unity. The library, located at the James Weldon Housing Project, was built by Capt Lewis and other police officers. Capt Lewis is **establishing libraries** at the remaining shelters and housing projects in the area. (Thousand Points of Light # 178, 25 June 1990)

∞ Mr. Albert Tonner, of Woodmere, New York, volunteers for the **Special Tutorial Education Program** (STEP), an initiative of the National Council of Jewish Women. Mr Tonner has tutored more than 60 third, fourth, and fifth grade students who are in need of academic support. For the last six years, he has met with eight to ten students each day at the Lawrence Public School #6, from 9:00 a.m. to 3:00 p.m., Monday through Thursday. Mr Tonner works one-on-one with the students, allowing him to focus on each of their specific needs. (Thousand Points of Light # 388, 25 Feb 1991)

∞ After witnessing a student retrieve a crumpled piece of paper from a garbage can and use it for his school work, Mr Nick Monreal, Jr., of San Antonio, Texas, realized that one cause of poor education performance in his community was the fact that many families could not afford to purchase school supplies for their children. In 1976, Mr Monreal founded **"Teach the Children,"** a program which provides school supplies for students from low income families. Volunteers from all segments of the community help plan and develop fundraising events, such as picnics, car washes, and local telethons. School supplies are then purchased and distributed to needy students who are identified by teachers and school counselors. (Thousand Points of Light #110, 6 April 1990)

∞ William Warner Johnson, a police officer of Washington, D.C. envisioned and **created a youth-oriented business center.** The Conner-Harris mini-mall, named after two victims of the drug war, started with a weight lifting room in Woodson Junior High School donated by Officer Johnson. He expanded the mall to include several stores that would cater to the consumer interests of youngsters. In addition, by allowing the students to operate the stores as their own businesses, they learn how to be junior entrepreneurs. The mini-mall, open after school and on weekends, serves as a teaching tool, whereby participants make their own products, such as T-shirts and craft items, and learn bookkeeping and marketing skills. (Thousand Points of Light #96, 21 Mar 1990)

∞ Mr. Viqar Shamin, of Hillsboro, Oregon, created **a computer program to assist his son in learning math**. After his son's mathematical skills greatly improved, Mr Shamin donated the program to an elementary school for use in math classes. Because the school did not have computers, Mr Shamin approached his employer, Intel Corporation, which donated fifteen obsolete computers and five printers. He spent a year installing the computers and now spends many mornings before work instructing teachers on the use of the software and ensuring that students are accustomed to the program's use. (Thousand Points of Light #326, 14 Dec. 1990)

For more information on how you can get involved and share with your school:

Books and Pamphlets:

Parental Involvement: Developing Networks Between School, Home, and Community by Sheila Wolfendale (Cassell, 1989)

Involving Parents in Schools by Sheila Wolfendale (Tycooly Publications, 1992)

SOS: Sustain Our Schools by Patricia Graham (Hill and Wang, 1992)

Save Our Schools: 66 Things You Can Do to Improve Your School Without Spending an Extra Penny by Mary S. Miller (Harper, 1993)

Involving Parents: A Handbook for Participation in Schools by P. Lyons (High Scope, 1984)

A Parent's Guide to Innovative Education: Working With Teachers, Schools, and Your Children for Real Learning by Ann W. Dodd (Noble Press, 1992)

Parents and Schools: A Sourcebook by Angela L. Carrasquillo and Clement B. London (Garland, 1993)

Parenting Our Schools: A Hands-on Guide to Educational Reform by Jill Bloom (Little, 1992)

"Parents: Partners in Education" (American Association of School Administrators, 1991)

Reaching for Excellence: An Effective Schools Sourcebook by Regina M. Kyle (U.S. Government Printing Office, 1985)

Organizations:

Points of Light Foundation
1737 H Street, NW
Washington, D.C. 20006
(202) 223-9186 or
1-800-59-LIGHT

American Association of Retired Persons
601 E. Street, NW
Washington, D.C. 20049

National Association of Partners in Education
209 Madison Street, Suit 401
Alexandria, VA 22314
(703) 836-4880

National Coalition for Parent Involvement in Education
P.O. Box 39
1201 - 16th Street, NW
Washington, D.C. 20036

11. Donate To Your Child's School

Time Cost:	1 hour a year
Resource Cost:	Zero

In addition to donating your time and skills in the classroom, you can consider donating assets that you have to your child's school. Donations in-kind, of physical assets or professional skills can be made by many of us. Some examples of the kinds of things schools can use include:

Globes	Computers
Maps (state, nation, and world)	Computer software
Sets of encyclopedias	Telephone instruments
World Almanacs	Modems
Dictionaries	Bookshelves
Posters (animals, educational)	Computer desks
Games	Child-sized furniture
Science kits and collections	Art materials
Easels	Children's chalkboards

Paint (art and indoor/outdoor)	Typewriters
Computer printers	Video equipment/videos
Adding machines & calculators	Photocopying machines
Computer paper and diskettes	Gardening equipment/seeds

For information on donating to your local school, contact your principal and school board, and your employer as well. For tax-deductable donations of old computers, contact **The National Cristina Foundation**, 42 Hillcrest Drive, Pelham Manor, NY 10803 or call 1-800-247-4784.

12. Give Teachers Gifts that Keep on Giving

Time Cost:	30 minutes a year
Resource Cost:	$5 to 25 annually

Around the holidays and the end of school, parents and students often give gifts to teachers. How many teachers have too many coffee mugs or Christmas tree ornaments? Think about giving your favorite teacher a gift that he or she will appreciate and use long after the holidays or the end of the school year. Some good ideas for teacher gifts include magazines, a coordinated gift from a local business or community group, or information on free educational materials. This year, consider giving something from the following listings of teacher-appropriate magazines and other interesting gift ideas.

∞ Magazine subscriptions for teachers:

The Educational Resources Information Center (ERIC) Review, free from ERIC/RCS, Indiana Research Center, Suite 150, 2805 East 10th Street, Bloomington, IN 47408-2698, or call 1-800-USE-ERIC (1-800-873-3742)

American Education, Supt of Documents, Washington., D.C. 20402

Education Digest, Prakken Publications, Inc, 275 Metty Drive, Suite 1, P.O. Box 8623, Ann Arbor, MI 48107

Education Summary, Croft Educational Services, 100 Garfield Avenue, New London, CT 06320

Education Product Report, Educ. Product Informational Exchange Institute, 463 West Street, New York, NY 10014

Learning: The Magazine for Creative Teaching, 530 University Avenue Palo Alto, CA 94301

Learning: Creative Ideas and Insights for Teachers, Springhouse Corporation, P.O. Box 54293-4293, Boulder, CO 80322

Options In Learning, Alliance for Parental Involvement in Education, P.O. Box 59, East Chatham, N.Y. 12060-0059

Phi Delta Kappan, P.O. Box 789, Bloomington, IN 47402

Resources in Education, Nat. Inst. of Education, 1200 19th Street, NW, Washington, D.C. 20208

Roeper Review: A Journal for Gifted Children, Roeper City and Country School, P.O. Box 329, Bloomfield Hills, MI 48013

School Product News, 614 Superior Ave West, Cleveland, OH 44113

Scholastic Parent and Child, Scholastic, Inc., 555 Broadway, New York, NY 10012

Teacher's College Record, Teacher's College, Columbia University, 525 W. 120th Street, New York, NY 10027

Teacher Magazine, Editorial Projects in Education, P.O. Box 2090, Marion, OH 43306

Teaching Pre-K through 8: The Professional Magazine for Teachers, Early Years, Inc, P.O. Box 54808, Boulder, CO 80327-4808

Today's Education, 1201 16th St, NW, Washington, D.C. 20036

Young Children, National Association for the Educations of Young Children,1834 Connecticutt Avenue, NW, Washington, D.C. 20009-5786

∞ Books for teachers that make great gifts include:

The Quality Teacher: Implementating Total Quality Management in the Classroom by Margaret Byrnes (Cornesky and Associates, 1992)

Teachers as Agents of Change: A New Look at School Improvement by Allan A. Glatthorm (National Education Association, 1993)

The New Teacher Almanac: The Complete Guide to Every Day of the School Year, Available from the Center for Applied Research in Education, Inc, P.O. Box 430, West Nyack, NY 10995

∞ If you can, talk to your employer about larger gifts for your school or child's classroom. Ideas for this can include:

> • Sending a teacher or teachers to professional workshops, seminars, in service training, etc. The availability of teacher professional development should be publicized not just internally, but to parents and the community as well. Many businesses are willing to subsidize training, transportation, donate materials, or even provide discounts in hotel rooms for an out of town workshop presenter, if only they knew about the possibility.

> • Use parent and community volunteers to set up free evening or weekend seminars to train teachers in things parents know. Topics that teachers can be trained in and benefit from include computers, software, networking, arts

and crafts, art appreciation, and science. Community groups, from industry panels, to environmental clubs, to hobbyist networks should target teachers for awareness projects.

• Photocopiers, computers, printers, typewriters, and supplies supporting them make great tax deductable donations from businesses.

• Repair contracts and services should be considered for donation to schools from local businesses. Copier or computer repair or maintenance, volunteer facility upgrade or repair work, photocopying and bindery services are all potential candidates for donatable effort, expertise, and value.

• Educational related carpets make great school and classroom gifts; Call the following sources for starters:

•• Flagship Carpets, call 1-800-848-4055

•• Smart Carpets, call 1-800-53-TEACH

•• Joy Carpets, call 1-800-645-2787

∞ <u>Free Science Video Programs</u>. The titles listed below are free to schools from **Karol Media**, 350 N. Pennsylvania Ave, P.O. Box 7600, Wilkes-Barre, PA 18773-7600 if requested by teachers or administrators. Does your school have and use the following educational materials?

• **The Challenge of the Unknown**: Seven 20 minute video programs about mathematics and problem solving for junior and senior high school students. Includes free teachers guide.

• **The Search for Solutions**: Nine 18 minute video programs about science and problem solving. Titles include Investigation, Evidence, Trial and Error, Patterns, Context, Modeling, Prediction, Adaptation, and Theory. Includes free teachers guide.

• **The American Enterprise Series**: Five 28 minute video programs about our economic history. Titles include Land, People, Innovation, Organization, and Government. Includes free teacher's guide.

∞ Ask your teacher or principal about National Diffusion Network (NDN) programs at your school. NDN is a federally funded system that makes exemplary educational programs available for adoption by schools, colleges, and other institutions. The NDN provides dissemination funds to exemplary programs, publicizes these programs, and trains and assistance to schools who want to adopt the programs. Sample programs available include:

• Elementary Level Programs

Conservation for Children
Hands On Elementary Science
Life Lab Science Program
Marine Science Project: FOR SEA
Starwalk

• Intermediate Level Programs

Informal Science Study
WIZE: Wildlife Inquiry through Zoo Education
Foundational Approaches in Science Teaching
Jeffco Life Science Program
Sci-Math
Science-Technology-Society: Preparing for Tomorrow's World
Stones and Bones: A Laboratory Approach to the Study of Biology, Modern Science, and Anthropology

• High School Level Programs

Geology Is
Mechanical Universe
PRISMS: Physics Resources and Instructional Strategies for Motivating Students
Physics - Teach to Learn

Write for NDN information to the Office of Educational Research and Improvement, National Diffusion Network, 555 New Jersey Avenue, NW, Washington, D.C. 20208-5684, or call: (202) 219-2134.

SECTION FOUR

ATTITUDES

The intangible, the invisible — the spirit of our approach— is probably the most important aspect of child-raising. Mistakes, large and small, are all forgiven in a child's eyes, but our attitudes are what they take with them forever. Can we change our attitudes? Do we change our moods, our outlook, and our goals? We do it all the time. I think, when we need to, we can also change our attitudes towards our own children and their actions within the family. The following section contains some ideas for attitude adjustment that are not too difficult, and might even be fun!

1. Learn Continually About Parenting

Time Cost:	30 minutes a week
Resource Cost:	Zero to $100

You continually learn new things as a parent. The key is to learn actively, rather than passively. While as a parent, you will meet and rise to the challenges facing you, there's a lot to be said for parental knowledge and preparedness. It just makes things easier. You should read whatever you can, and share with other parents (of all ages) your questions and concerns. Some ideas are:

∞ Ask for a "Parent's Section" in local and school libraries—a bookshelf or corner in the library specifically devoted to educational information for parents and caretakers. Most libraries already have a variety of books that would be helpful to parents and caretakers of children, but they are not displayed or organized to promote their use by the target audience. Books for the parent section may be already available in the library, and donations should also be solicited. Consider asking the community for donations, and setting up a parent focused book shelf in the libraries for bookswaps.

Note: Don't limit this concept to libraries alone. Anywhere parents congregate and convene, such as child care centers, social service agencies, or "Moms and Tots" get-togethers can be locations to make parenting resources available. Ask the question and offer to help!

∞ Contact the Home and School Institute. This non-profit organization dedicated to "helping families build children's achievement in school and beyond," has created a "Parent's Shelf." For a total of $50.00 plus $6.00 for shipping and handling, individuals, school libraries, and businesses may purchase a set of highly acclaimed Home and School Institute titles. The set includes:

• *MegaSkills: How Families Can Help Children Succeed in School and Beyond.* (48 page handbook, pre-kindergarten through grade 8)

• *Job Success Begins at Home.* (Six booklets, 96 pages, grades 4-9)

• *Bright Idea.* (112 pages, kindergarten through grade 8)

• *Families Learning Together.* (96 pages, kindergarten through grade 6)

• *Get Smart: Advice for Teens with Babies.* (40 pages, junior and senior high school level)

• *Survival Guide for Busy Parents.* (80 pages, kindergarten through grade 6)

• *Careers and Caring.* (64 pages, pre-kindergarten through grade 6)

• *Special Solutions: Extra Help Activities.* (176 pages, kindergarten through grade 6)

• *101 Activities for More Effective School-Community Involvement.* (80 pages)

• *MegaSkills: English / Spanish Parent Handbook.* (96 pages)

∞ Share with other parents, and help them learn about parenting. Some examples that focus on parental learning include the following:

• HIPPY is "Home Instruction Program for Preschool Youngsters" and was first implemented in Israel. It is a program of instruction for parents that enables them to tutor their preschool children. A HIPPY program requires training for parents/caretakers, and requires fifteen minutes of daily tutoring by the parent with the children in their home. Arkansas has implemented HIPPY, and calculates the cost of around $750 per student, and clear academic benefits have already been noted. Funding for the program was arranged through the Job Training Partnership Act and other state funding. Write for information to HIPPY USA, 53 West 23 Street, New York, New York 10010.

• Shirley Mosinger founded "Beginning Babies with Books" in 1990. Through this effort, every new mother at the St Louis Regional Medical Center, many of whom are low-income teenagers, receive books free of charge. Only ten volunteers serve over 3,500 new mothers each year. They visit mothers in the hospital to discuss with them how reading develops a child's interest in learning. They also offer advice on how to read to children. (Thousand Points of Light # 512, 18 July 1991)

• The Variety Pre-Schooler's Workshop, of Syosset, New York was founded in 1966 to provide a wide variety of services for families and their children, who have learning, language or behavioral difficulties. The volunteers, many of whom are parents, seniors and high school students, assist the staff with teaching children good study habits and communication skills. The workshop has expanded to include a family center, an early childhood development program, and a parent education and guidance program. (Thousand Points of Light # 523, 31 July 1991)

• Project Love, in Bartow, Florida, was founded in 1989 by former teacher Ann Thayer as a summer enrichment program for students in Hispanic migrant communities. Today, Project

Love's "Morning with Moms" program helps women learn good parenting skills, improve their reading abilities, and obtain high school General Equivalency Diplomas. Those mothers who babysit children of high-school age mothers also have the opportunity to learn while they volunteer. In between regular classes, high school staff members teach mothers about art, health, and reading so they are better prepared to reinforce their children's learning at home. In addition, through Project Love, volunteers "adopt" migrant families, clean up old teddy bears for elementary school students, and refurbish homes in need of repair. (Thousand Points of Light 674, 22 Jan 1992)

For additional information:

The Home & School Institute
MegaSkills Education Center
1201 16th Street, NW
Washington, D.C. 20036
(202) 466-3633

Institute for American Values
250 West 57 Street Suite 2415
New York, NY 10107
(212) 246-3942

Family Resource Council
700 13th Street, NW, Suite 1180
Washington, D.C. 20005
(202) 293-2100

Family Resource Coalition
200 South Michigan Ave., Suite 1520
Chicago, IL 60604-2404
(312) 341-0900

American Association of Parents and Children
560 Herndon Parkway, Suite 110
Herndon, VA 22070

National Parenting Association
P.O. Box 20280
Bloomington, MN 55420

National Parenting Service   (Touch tone phone service, 24 hrs/day
1-900-246-MOMS $1.95 first min./.95 each minute thereafter)

Work-Family Directions   (Offers a telephone service to companies;
930 Commonwealth Avenue   Employees can call to get information
Boston, MA 02215-1274   on how to motivate and solve learning
(617) 278-4000   problems, and select schools.

2. Keep "Damage" In Perspective

Time Cost:	None
Resource Cost:	None

We parents have a lot of responsibility, and what we do (or don't do) impacts our children. We have to consider seriously what we call "the good" and what we call "the bad." For many of us, the concept of "damage" is a driving factor in how we parent. Whether because of our own childhood memories of mistakes made, and parents enraged or disappointed, or our present-day concerns about mistakes we or our children may be making, the idea and definition of damage must be dealt with. I would suggest that many times we say things to our children and also to ourselves that are damning, hurtful, and hateful simply because we feel that some kind of long-term damage has been effected. For the record, here are some things that do **NOT** constitute "damage":

- Crayon marks on the wall
- Picking one's nose or thumb-sucking in public

- Food spilled on one's best outfit
- Nicks, scratches, or scrapes on the furniture
- Jumping on beds
- Turning lights on and off
- Playing music loudly
- Minor accidents that don't require special attention
- Messy bedrooms
- Leaving personal property in the living room
- Not putting dirty clothes in the hamper (or putting clean clothes in the hamper)
- Spilled milk

This is just for starters. When faced with a questionable act that you feel might warrant a cruel, hurtful, or sarcastic outburst, ask yourself these two questions:

1) What the action inherently dangerous?

2) Will it matter in twenty years?

If the action is dangerous, you as guardian need to act to prevent future occurrence. If the act will have serious effects twenty years from now (i.e. your five year old wants to change citizenship to Fiji or Iceland), then perhaps your parental sterness should come to bear. But otherwise, chill!

These questions also apply to how you judge yourself or your spouse. As larger, heavier, and perhaps more frustrated children than our kids, we parents have the potential to be physically dangerous. If we have become physically dangerous to our kids, we need to stop no matter what. And we really should be kind, gentle and loving. When we as parents make mistakes, we must also learn to forgive ourselves, asking whether the one instance of our poor judgement will matter in twenty years.

3. Establish Family History With Your Children

Time Cost:	4-8 hours a year
Resource Cost:	Zero to $100 annually

One thing that every family should do is keep and develop family histories. Most of us keep pictures in boxes or photo albums. We have an address book somewhere, and we know a little about our grandparents and relatives. This raw material is ideal fodder for development into something just a little better, and it is an ideal family project to pursue over time. The keeping of family histories, pictoral and written, takes a little time, but provides endless enjoyment, especially for children, as they muse through photo albums and see and understand their own history. Some ideas to enhance your family's sense of "family history" include:

∞ Get a large binder, scrapbook, or photo album (or maybe all three). Sit down with other family members and fill it up!

• Try to label or mark the more important of your pictures with a date, a location, and a "who" if applicable. If you can't place some of it, check with some of your relatives who might know, but try to identify whatever you can and record it.

• Keep old documents or letters nearby as well, to include in the album. Consider including anything that might have sentimental or historical value — a pressed flower, a deed, or a sketch.

• Think about preparing a notebook or scrapbook for each member of the family, and for different family events, like trips, reunions, or special family events. This collection can be the basis for not only a lot of fun, but the creation of a sense of continuity for the family.

∞ In addition to pictoral collections, poems, cards and letters, newspaper clippings of interest, musings and journals of family members should also be kept. Private journals should be private, but the keeping of a public journal for either individuals or the family as a whole should be encouraged. Perhaps an open family logbook, where each member of the family can write down whatever he or she wants can be kept out in the family room, available for all for review and input.

∞ Play twenty questions with your kids, and when you get together with grandparents and other relatives. Record on tape or video, if you think of it. Some questions to have your children ask:

• How did you meet (Mom, Dad, Grandma, Grandpa)?

• Where did you go on your first date?

• What was the first thing you noticed about (Mom, Dad, Grandma, Grandpa)?

• What was school like when you were in my grade?

• What was the craziest thing you ever did as a kid? The silliest thing? The scariest thing?

• How did you celebrate birthdays when you were a kid?

• How did you celebrate (Christmas, Thanksgiving, Independence Day) when you were a kid?

• What kind of house(s) did you live in when you were a kid?

• What was your favorite story or book when you were a kid?

• What kind of car did you first learn to drive?

• Did you have a pet? What was it like?

• When was the first time you rode on a train? On an airplane? On a ship or boat?

• How old were you when you left home?

• What was your first job? Your most interesting job?

∞ Put pictures, newspaper clippings, and certificates for family members on display on hallway, living room, and bedroom walls. We sometimes joke about "I love me" walls in our boss's office, but a great place for these displays is in our homes where we can see them and feel good.

∞ Create and use family newsletters during holidays and birthdays. Try creating with your child a newsletter-type birthday card that summarizes the child's previous year as a way of recording history and putting events in perspective.

∞ Attend family reunions whenever you can.

Further information on family histories and research is available from the following organizations:

Institute of Family History & Genealogy
21 Hanson Avenue
Somerville, MA 02143
(617) 666-0877

Genealogical Institute
P.O. Box 22045
Salt Lake City, UT 84122
(801) 532-3327

4. Allow Your Child 3 "Bad" Habits

Time Cost:	None
Resource Cost:	None

We parents tend to be concerned about things that probably aren't so important in the long run. We are often unknowlingly more concerned about the transitory than the long-term. A prime example of this is how we nag incessantly for our children to pick up, clean up, stop nose-picking, stop looking cross-eyed, ad nauseum. We think the "transitory" situation is important enough to be nagged about, but for the child, the "permanent" situation is the *state of being nagged*. In fact, the negative effects of being nagged will stay with the child much longer than the individual "bad habit" ever could. To eliminate this time-wasting habit, we need to draw the line on what is transitory and what is not, and dole out our nagging accordingly. To assist you, here is the short list of things we really don't need to nag our children about (I call them "bad habit freebies"):

Bad Habit Freebies:

- Nose-picking
- Ear pulling or poking (one's own ear, not one's neighbor's)
- Not cleaning one's bedroom (beyond minimal safety standards)
- Thumb and finger sucking
- Drinking out of the milk or juice container
- Leaving the toilet seat up (although this is borderline)
- Not flushing the toilet every time
- Not replacing the toilet paper roll
- Not putting all their dirty clothes in the hamper
- Leaving toothpaste lids off
- Hair twisting
- Not refilling ice cube trays
- Placing empty juice or milk containers back in the fridge
- Leaving wet towels on the floor
- Not putting books back on the bookshelf
- Leaving toys out in the family room

If you look at the habits listed above as "freebies," a common thread emerges. All these bad, annoying habits are exhibitions of discourtesy to the rest of the family. In fact, it is their discourteous nature that really makes us mad, even more than the act itself. But the way to instill courtesy in the discourteous is to first exhibit courtesy yourself toward the children, and then insist on courtesy in the simplest of ways. This way, courteous behavior can be developed in the child from within, and the bad habit freebies will eventually go away. (Or else in eighteen years, the child will move out— either way there's hope). Consider posting a list of required courtesies prominently throughout the house. The list may include:

- Please (used frequently, as a modifier)
- Thank You (see "Please")
- May I (this occurs before the grab, never during or after)
- Excuse me (used when leaving the table or bumping someone)

Notice that the courtesy list is much shorter and much easier to implement. You may need to "nag" with these phrases, but if you insist, your children will soon form good habits. When your children habitually repeat these and other courteous phrases, eventually, these words will have a subliminal positive influence on the bad habits and other rude behaviors. At least you'll have some good behavior to balance some of the bad habits. Over time, courtesy will impact the overall climate in your home and you'll notice things going more smoothly.

5. Cultivate Peaceful Responses

Time Cost:	2 minutes a day
Resource Cost:	None

Just as our children need to learn to have some automatic responses such as "Please," "Thank You," and "Excuse Me," we parents need to cultivate some polite, automatic responses to our kids as well. There is one simple rule to these responses, and the rule is "What would Grandmother say?" The "grandmother" I have in mind is not necessarily your mother or grandmother, but the imaginary grandmother who bakes cookies, and knits sweaters, and always has a hug and time for you. This grandmother with the right answers is the nurturer in all of us. We may feel we don't have much nurturer in us, but the very reason we have kids (and marvel at the joy they bring us) is because these kids bring out that "nurturer" inside us. So let's let it happen! Listed below are some sample situations to review as we develop the "grandmother response:"

Example 1. Your child shows up at the door on a cold afternoon of playing. Her coat is missing a button (it wasn't before) and her mittens are gone, her fingers freezing. You say:

a) I told you before to never take off your mittens! Now they're lost, and look at your coat!....

b) Come here, sweetheart, and let me warm you up. You've been gone so long I started to miss you!

Example 2. Your two kids have been arguing and teasing all day, and then you hear a crash. A loud furniture-sounding crash, and then silence, and then a high pitched wail. The smaller kid is a little shaken and something liquid is all over the living room floor. You:

a) Run screaming marginal obscenities into the living room, then continue to yell while pointing at the mess. Both children are sent to their bedroom, possibly running away from you as you try to get a hand on them.

b) You sit quietly wherever you are and wait for at least one kid to explain to you what happened (or quietly clean up the mess). When you have an idea of what happened, and are confident you can survey the scene without making one, check it out. Then send the children to their rooms separately, or give them a situationally-appropriate work detail together.

Example 3. Your adorable child will not eat dinner. He doesn't like it. It's not good. Plus he is whi-i-i-i-i-ning about it. You:

a) Tell him in a loud and demanding voice that he is sitting there until his plate is clean if it takes all night. You may even suggest that it will be breakfast if he waits long enough.

b) Explain that he doesn't have to eat it, or eat it all, but consumption of dessert or after dinner snacks depends on it. Offer to have him make himself a peanut butter sandwich to eat instead. Change the subject, and don't worry about it. If whining persists, ask the child to go elsewhere, as whining is not conducive to the family's collective digestion.

The "grandmotherly" response is normally a good, loving, and non-controlling response, and it tends to bring out the best in the child with limited ill effects. Life itself contains painful lessons for all of us, and while we parents feel that we are protecting or assisting our children through life with our demands and warnings, the best thing we can do is raise our child to be open to new ideas and experiences, with a sense of personal control and self-determination. What I mean is a sense of competence — competence that allows our children to learn life's lessons positively and with love for others and him or herself.

Erma Bombeck wrote a wonderful column once about the ways we treat visiting guests versus the way we treat our children. It was wonderfully and wittily made clear that if we treated guests as we treat our kids we would soon have no guests. Think about it!

For more information, read:

Self-Esteem: The Key to Your Child's Well-Being by Reynold Bean and Harris Clemes (Zebra, 1982)

52 Simple Ways to Build Your Child's Self Esteem by Jan Dargaty (Oliver-Nelson, 1991)

The Magic of Encouragement: Nurturing Your Child's Self-Esteem by Stephanie Marston (Morrow, 1990)

6. Pursue Your Own Interests

Time Cost:	1 hour a week (minimum)
Resource Cost:	Zero to several thousand dollars a year

Parenthood is not prison, but another stage in your own growth. Even early parenthood, with it corresponding regrets and personal sacrifices, need not be a heavy weight on your personal life. Every parent should try to spend time on his or her personal interests. If your work is your passion, you set an excellent example for your child of diligence, satisfaction in achievement, and productivity. If you have a artistic or creative hobby, or a a favorite athletic activity, or a collection of any sort, you should pursue these interests. Find a way to do so, possibly involving your children at certain times. If you fail to pursue your passions because of (or even partly because of) your children, the sense of subtle resentment will be far more damaging than the time spent away from the house, or time spent not cleaning the house, or not preparing six-course meals. The key is balance — certainly if you'd like to spend every waking hour on your hobby, but you have a job and a home with children, then allocate your time rationally, on a long-term calendar.

You have each child for eighteen years at home (as a general rule). Your job may last for a longer or shorter period, depending on what you like or want or need to do. Your hobby and your interests can likewise last varying lengths of time. Think about what you and your family need, and work out an informal long term plan to satisfy all your needs. Make room for your dreams, and spend time pursuing them even while your children are young. You will all benefit.

7. Spend Less Money

Time Cost:	20 minutes a week
Resource Cost:	Zero to $30 annually

his suggestion may seem strange in a book about what you can do for your children, but it isn't really. Our natural desire to conserve our resources is suppressed by the pressure of sales pitches for toys and clothes, no time to cook, and the driving need for entertainment to relieve the stress of parenting.

We should probably save about five percent of our after-tax pay for each child in the household. This is over and above the amount you save for your own retirement, vacations, a home, a car, or your annual tax bill. Commit to doing this early on for each of your children, and set up bank or mutual fund accounts with automatic deposit arrangements.

Saving more and spending less are educational for your children. For example:

∞ Your kids get used to thinking of acquiring things in terms of tradeoffs — they understand budgeting because they see it every day.

∞ By reducing your consumption of "new" things, specifically convenience items and energy, you are contributing to the ecological health of your community and the earth.

∞ Your kids will retain their native non-materialistic values, and be less susceptable to peer pressures towards "ownership" of "things."

For more information on living cheaply and saving money:

Books:

Your Money or Your Life: Transforming Your Realationship With Money and Achieving Financial Independence by Joe Dominguez with Vicki Robin (Viking-Penguin Books, 1992)

Living Cheaply with Style by Ernest Callenbach (Ronin Publications, 1993)

How to Pinch a Penny Till It Screams: How to Stretch Your Dollar in the Nineties by Rochelle L. McDonald (Avery Park, 1993)

The Tightwad Gazette by Amy Dacyczyn (Villard Books, 1993)

Newsletters:

Cheapskate Monthly   *The Tightwad Gazette*
Box 2135   RR #1 Box 3750
Paramount, CA 90723   Leeds, ME 04263
(310) 630-8845   (207) 524-7962

Living Cheap News
P.O. Box 700058
San Jose, CA 95170
(408) 257-1680

Skinflint News
Box 818
Palm Harbor, FL 34682
1-800-496-8672

The Penny Pincher
P.O. Box 809
King's Park, NY 11754-0809
1-800-41-PENNY

8. Share Humor

Time Cost:	5 minutes a day
Resource Cost:	None

It has been reported that children laugh about 400 times a day, but by the time they become adults, they are down to only fifteen laughs a day! Where did all our laughter go? Children tend to be happy and full of humor, humorous observations, and jokes, until we curb this social behavior to fit our own sensibilities. Some curbing is part of growing up, but a lot of what we try to keep down in our children is their simple exuberance and joyful "putting together" of the mysteries of human experience. Humor is a way to make sense of it all, and it needs to be encouraged and nurtured in our children so that it will be retained fully and satisfactorily in happy adults.

Some ideas for encouraging humor in the family include:

∞ Short-story lines around the dinner table — where one family member starts a story and each person gets a turn at adding the next sentence or sentences to the story.

∞ Check out joke and humor books from the library.

∞ Read humor columns in your daily paper out loud at the dinner table

∞ Post a cartoon of the day or week on the refrigerator and/or bulletin board.

∞ Learn and do magic tricks after dinner

∞ Play "What if?" games during and after dinner.

∞ Instead of asking what the child or the adult has done at school or at work that day, try a guessing game. For example, "Let me guess what you did at school today...."

• You caught an alligator that had escaped from the science class, and rode to McDonald's on its back, or....

• You taught the class instead of the teacher, and the teacher missed three questions on the pop quiz you gave....

• You sang a song to the English class, and....

∞ Have color-themed dinners — for example, green dyed scrambled eggs, green macaroni and cheese, green salad, spinach, green butter for the bread, and green jello or cake. Let the kids do the coloring with food colors, and you will be laughing, too.

∞ Have a food fight (outdoors) or set up one night a month for "Viking Night" — where no one uses utensils, just hands and fingers.

∞ Play "sausages". One person is the victim and all others must ask him or her questions, to which he or she can only reply "sausages." The object is to make the victim laugh. The player whose question causes laughter becomes the next victim. Words referring to food items other than "sausages" can be substituted.

Conclusion

You can have super kids in thirty minutes a day—but, after trying some of the ideas discussed in this book, you will probably find yourself having more fun with them and spending more time with them (and spending less time on whatever it was that you did before). Perhaps that is the real goal of this book. Enjoy!

Photo by Marvin Shavers

Karen U. Kwiatkowski, M.S., M.A.

About The Author

Karen U. Kwiatkowski, M.S., M.A. is an Air Force officer, stationed at Aviano AB, Italy. In her twelve years with the United States Air Force, she has moved five times. She has lived in Fairbanks, Alaska; Boston, Massachusetts; Madrid, Spain, and Fiume Veneto, Italy. She has earned a master of science in science management from the University of Alaska and a master of liberal arts in government from Harvard University.

Karen has taught short courses in Total Quality Management and facilitated Air Force quality teams. She recently won a prize in an international essay contest on world-wide arms reduction.

She has been married for thirteen years to Hap Kwiatkowski, and together they have four children, ages three to ten years. Hap has stayed home full time with the children for the last nine years. This non-traditional experience of parenting four children while moving frequently has been unique and educational.

Karen has researched parenting and educational issues for the last five years and *Super Kids In 30 Minutes A Day* reflects her experience. She has been involved in parent-teacher organizations and has edited and published newsletters for military and educational groups. She currently resides in Fiume Veneto, Italy, near Aviano Air Base, near Venice.

Books Available From Robert D. Reed Publishers
750 La Playa, Suite 647 • San Francisco, CA 94121
Telephone: (800) PR-GREEN Fax: (408) 255-8830

Title/Author	Price	Quantity	Subtotal

Super Kids In 30 Minutes A Day by Karen U. Kwiatkowski
ISBN 1-885003-06-4 $9.95   _____   _____

**Healing Our Schools: A Parents' And Teachers' Guide
For Improving Education** by Steven P. Mitchell
ISBN 1-885003-08-0 $11.95   _____   _____

50 Things You Can Do About Guns by James M. Murray
ISBN 1-885003-00-5 $7.95   _____   _____

**Get Out Of Your Thinking Box: 365 Ways To Brighten
Your Life & Enhance Your Creativity** by Lindsay Collier
ISBN 1-885003-01-3 $7.95   _____   _____

**The Funeral Book: How To Save Money And Reduce
Stress While Planning A Funeral** by C. W. Miller
ISBN 1-885003-02-1 $7.95   _____   _____

**Lovers & Survivors: A Partner's Guide To Living With &
Loving A Sexual Abuse Survivor** by S. Y. de Beixedon, Ph.D.
ISBN 1-885003-09-9 $14.95   _____   _____

**Healing Is Remembering Who You Are: A Guide For
Healing Your Mind, Your Emotions, And Your Life**
by Marilyn Gordon, CCH (Certified Clinical Hypnotherapist)
ISBN 1-885003-10-2 $11.95   _____   _____

Books Available From Robert D. Reed Publishers

Title/Author	Price	Quantity	Subtotal

500 Tips For Coping With Chronic Illness by P. D. Jacobs
ISBN 1-885003-04-8 $9.95   _____   _____

Live To Be 100+: Healthy Choices For Maximizing Your
Life by Richard Deeb
ISBN 1-885003-07-2 $11.95   _____   _____

To order books from Robert D. Reed Publishers:
Please fill out forms and return them with payment for all orders.

Single books are priced as listed. Additional copies are discounted.
(You may order any combination of books to receive discount.)
- 1 to 5 books (list price)
- 6 to 10 books (10% off list price)
- 11 and more books (25% off list price)

For larger orders, contact the publisher for special discounts.

Please include payment and postage with all orders:
$2.50 for first book (S&H) & $1.00 for each additional book.
(California residents, add 8.5% sales tax.)
Please send me books marked for a total cost of $_____.

Ship Books To My Address Below:

Name: _____

Organization: _____

Address: _____

City: _____ State: ____ Zip: _____

Telephone: _____ Fax: _____

Order books from the publisher: Robert D. Reed

750 La Playa, Suite 647 • San Francisco, CA 94121

Telephone: 800-PR-GREEN • Fax: (408) 255-8830

(OK To Photocopy This Order Form)

To order additional copies of:
Super Kids In 30 Minutes A Day by Karen U. Kwaitkowski
(ISBN 1-885003-06-4)

Please fill out the form below.
Return it with payment for all orders. Thank you.

Send me _____ copies for a total cost of $_____.

Costs: $9.95 each, plus $2.50 for first book (S&H)
& $1.00 for each additional copy.
(California residents, add 8.5% sales tax.)
Save on larger orders!
Order 5 copies for $39.95 and get Free shipping.
Order 10 copies for only $69.95 and get Free shipping.
Special pricing for large orders. Contact publisher.

Ship Books To My Address Below:

Name: _____

Organization: _____

Address: _____

City: _____ State: _____ Zip: _____

Telephone: _____ Fax: _____

Order Books From The Publisher:

Robert D. Reed

750 La Playa, Suite 647 • San Francisco, CA 94121
Telephone: 1-800-PR-GREEN

(Note: we are now accepting quality manuscripts.)